W9-CES-976

Ex
Libris

Lowell R. Kantzer

Donald G. Bloesch

The Invaded Church

Other Books by Donald G. Bloesch

Centers of Christian Renewal
The Christian Life and Salvation
The Crisis of Piety
The Christian Witness in a Secular Age
Christian Spirituality East and West (co-author)
The Reform of the Church
The Ground of Certainty
Servants of Christ (editor)
The Evangelical Renaissance
Wellsprings of Renewal
Light a Fire

Donald G. Bloesch
The Invaded Church

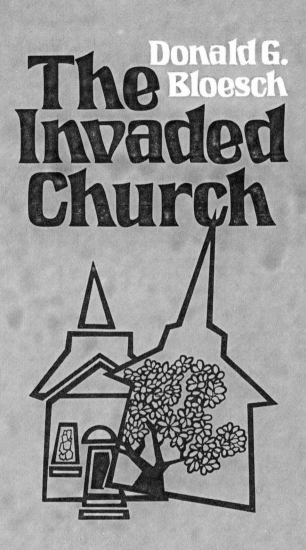

Word Books, Publisher

Waco, Texas

94020

THE INVADED CHURCH

Copyright © 1975, by Word, Incorporated, Waco, Texas. All rights reserved. No part of this book may be reproduced in any form, except for brief quotations in reviews, without the written permission of the publisher.

Printed in the United States of America.

Library of Congress catalog number: 74–27487

To
Richard John Bloesch
my brother

Contents

Preface

The theme of this collection of essays, some of which were delivered as lectures on various occasions, is the present crisis facing the church. This, in my judgment, is a spiritual crisis, a crisis of faith. It is manifested in the loss of the transcendent. It is reflected too in a new Christology which effectively denies the deity of Christ and in a new eschatology which rules out supernatural intervention at the end of history. Those who examine this book carefully will see that it offers little solace to the political right wing, even though the dominant critique is aimed at the theologies of liberation and revolution.

I have felt for some time that a protest must be lodged against the naturalistic monistic perspective that has infiltrated the theology and worship of the church today. I cannot go along with Joseph Mathews of the Ecumenical Institute who has declared that "when you talk about the Other World, you are dealing with the ordinary secular world and the ordinary secular consciousness of man." Nor can I share the view of Andrew Greeley that religious truth has to do with a reality hidden in human life rather than the revelation of a transcendent reality in human history. It was out of a concern to reaffirm the supernatural and transcendent dimensions of the faith that this book was written.

I acknowledge my indebtedness to Karl Barth and Jacques Ellul, who in their social involvement have sought to maintain the distinctions between the heavenly and the earthly, the sacred and the secular. But I have also been greatly influenced by the political realism of the Protestant Reformers and of Reinhold Niebuhr. The doctrine of the two kingdoms found in both Calvin and Luther cannot be summarily dismissed. We need to rediscover the reality of what Luther

9

called the kingdom of the world, a kingdom of darkness that has infiltrated both church and state and which constitutes the major threat to the faith in every age. Far from endorsing a privatized religion I believe that we as Christians must do all within our power to change oppressive social conditions. In addition I contend that because even we Christians still have one foot in the old aeon, it is incumbent upon us to participate in the political process in order to keep the destructive forces within man and society in check. In contrast to Ellul and Vernard Eller I do not hold to an absolute pacifist position, but I am sympathetic to their emphasis on maintaining a Christian identity in our social involvement. With Calvin we seek a holy commonwealth in which the law of God would be dominant in the secular as well as the religious realm. But such a community would by no means be a social utopia but at the most only a broken sign and witness of the perfect kingdom of righteousness that is still coming.

Acknowledgments

I am grateful to the *Reformed Review* for permission to republish my essay "The Missing Dimension" (Chapter IV) which appeared in the Spring, 1973, issue of that magazine. I also wish to thank *Christianity Today* for permitting the republication of "Burying the Gospel" (Chapter II), which appeared in the September 24 and October 8 issues of that journal (in 1971). This article has been reworked and greatly expanded. A word of appreciation is also extended to *His* magazine for granting permission for the reprinting of Chapter I, which was published in abridged form in the February and March issues of 1975.

Finally the Brunnen-Verlag in Giessen, Germany, has been very kind to permit the republication of the last paragraph in my essay "Rethinking the Church's Mission," which is a chapter in the book *Berufung und Bewährung,* a Festschrift in honor of Erick Wickberg, the recently retired general of the Salvation Army. This paragraph forms the conclusion of my last chapter, "How Christians Can Change the World."

Chapters III and IV were originally given in abbreviated form as the David Nyvall lectures at North Park Seminary in Chicago in the spring of 1972.

Introduction

In this book I seek to document the thesis that there is a church conflict and that it is growing. I try to point a pathway to reconciliation but at the same time show where reconciliation is not possible.

The growing church conflict has to be understood against the background of two clashing theologies or perspectives on life. On the one hand is the historic faith of the church given new impetus in a resurgent evangelicalism, and on the other is a new modernism which tends to accommodate the faith to worldly values. This latest theological current places heaven in the continuum of history and sees a just society as more important than personal salvation. The new theology has taken various forms: some strands emphasize political liberation and worldly hope while others seem more concerned with the quest for mystical experience and the discovery of wonder. Both political theology and neo-mysticism reflect a naturalistic world view, since they tend to deny or play down the incursion of the supernatural into worldly history. This is not true of all forms of political and liberation theology, but even those which are more Christocentric are accustomed to speak of salvation through politics and a kingdom of promise through social revolution. As the lines between the two mentalities become more clear-cut, some political theologians who try to relate to biblical faith may have to rethink their positions and move one way or the other.

In contrast to the secular and political theologies a new evangelical theology has arisen which places a special emphasis on the supernatural aspects of the faith without neglecting the social dimension. It also upholds the Bible as the primal authority for faith as over against empirical

13

experience or mystical vision. The evangelical wind can be discerned in Roman Catholicism as well as in mainline Protestantism. While some aspects of this movement are reactionary both politically and theologically, others bear the earmarks of genuine biblical and spiritual renewal.

The polarization in the church currently revolves about the precise relation of the church to society. In this book I shall speak to this important problem, not necessarily to resolve the division in the church but to sharpen it. I shall try to point to where the real issues lie.

We need again to discover that Christianity is a revolutionary religion and that the gospel is a stick of dynamite in the social matrix. But this does not mean that social action is the mission of the church, though it may be a faithful expression of the faith of the church. Christianity is revolutionary because it transforms the values and hopes of men and engenders a style of life that goes counter to prevailing mores. Too often, unfortunately, Christians have not acted as a revolutionary spiritual force in society but instead have become immersed in questionable forms of politics or have sought to cultivate an ethereal spirituality which is no longer related to ordinary life.

There is a need today to integrate faith and life, theology and the secular disciplines of knowledge. Many conservative Christians assent to the biblical fundamentals, but in the areas of economics and politics they hold quite secular views. They may lead lives of exemplary devotion, but they accept uncritically the latest findings and fashions of the educationists and social scientists.

If we are to recover an evangelical catholic faith, we must avoid a simple gospel reductionism. I concur with Harvie M. Conn of Westminster Seminary that we must stress "the priestly manifestation of God's mercy in love and healing" as well as "a prophetic witness to Christ's redemption." We must also go on to emphasize "the kingly demonstration of Christ's Lordship over politics, society and the world."[1] In our mandate to bring the whole world in subjection to Christ we may very well be accused of triumphalism, and when this takes the form of a religious or churchly imperialism then we must indeed beware. At the same time there is a triumphalism in the gospel itself, and we must not hesitate to carry the claims of the gospel into the uttermost parts of the world.

I consider myself somewhat of a political liberal or at least a moderate. I am concerned that the church not remain aloof from the social crisis today, but I also seek for a deeper theological undergirding in its social involvement. As Ellul maintains:

> The Church ought not . . . to justify the world's solution, but it ought to find its own way, given it by God, which it alone can follow. It is only on this condition that the Church will cease to be a sociological movement, and be present in the world with the effectiveness given by the Holy Spirit.[2]

My thesis is that the real division in the church is not between evangelism and social action but between the secular humanism of our technological society, which has infiltrated the church, and the transcendent claims of the holy, catholic faith. A "technocratic liberalism" (Robert Bellah) in which man is seen as master and controller of nature and history is challenging the theocentricism of our religious heritage. When such a mood or ideology appears in a religious guise, as in evolutionary religious naturalism, then there is a threat to the church from within.

In my estimation there is today a need for a confessing church that will testify to its faith before the world and thereby sharpen the distinctions between the church and the world. The enemy is not simply collectivism or nationalism or a new Baalism but a secular or worldly Christianity which has accepted at least in part the values and goals of the surrounding society. When secular values however praiseworthy are uncritically adopted by the church as authentically or even potentially Christian, the tension between the transcendent Word of God and human culture is lost sight of, and the result is a compromised version of the faith. In Germany the Barmen Confession was aimed primarily at the German Christians, those who sought to amalgamate the faith and the values and precepts of National Socialism. A confessing church would stand against both a diluted liberalism, which sometimes takes the form of a compulsive social activism, and cultural fundamentalism, which tends toward a privatistic religiosity. It would see a biblically based social action as a worthwhile demonstration of our faith but not as the message of the faith.

The task of the church today is to make people homesick for another world, to uproot their attachments to this world. The secular realm is not the total realm but the realm of man's achievements. Christianity must permeate the realm of the secular with redemptive influence. But how it does this and with what goals in mind is now a subject of debate. This is where the growing church conflict is most clearly visible, though its roots are in widely disparate metaphysical visions that cannot be harmonized.

NOTES

1. See *The Presbyterian Journal*, Vol. XXI, No. 9 (Jan. 24, 1973), p. 9.

2. Jacques Ellul, *The Presence of the Kingdom*, trans. Olive Wyon (New York: Seabury Press, 1967), 2nd printing, p. 152.

The Church which does not ask itself whether it is not threatened by apostasy, and therefore in need of renewal, should beware lest it become a sleeping and sick Church, even sick unto death.

Karl Barth

Between the man who is bound to a God in heaven, and another who knows nothing of this bond, there is a contrast deeper than all other contrasts which separate man from man. Men of the two camps can never reach any real unity, even if they are fighting side by side for the same earthly gains.

Karl Heim

No less is at stake here than the unity of the Church. . . . The cleavage in the understanding of the Gospel can be so deep as to drive us to Luther's words about "two churches," the Church of God and the church of the anti-Christ.

Helmut Gollwitzer

Evangelicals and the World Council of Churches . . . have very different viewpoints, and I don't see how they can be reconciled. Basic issues make for basic clashes. Big protests are not fashionable now, but the whole *raison d'être* of the [Lausanne] congress reflects that the World Council is not giving the leadership it should on the central issue of expressing our faith. If there is no Gospel heart, there is no future for the church.

Kenneth Hamilton

1

A Church Divided

*If I am not totally deceived, we are right in the middle of
a struggle for the faith, of a* Kirchenkampf [*church struggle*]
compared to which the Kirchenkampf *under the Nazis was
only a skirmish.*

HERMANN DIETZFELBINGER

Despite the varied attempts at reconciliation there is no
doubt that the church today is torn by growing polarization.
Frederick Herzog in his *Theology of the Liberating Word*
speaks of a new church conflict and criticizes both the secular and black theologies for accommodating the gospel to
the spirit of the culture. While I do not entirely agree with
the way in which Herzog delineates this conflict, I certainly
concur in his judgment that such a conflict is emerging.

A popular misinterpretation is to see this division in the
church as between socially conservative laymen and a coterie
of enlightened clergy. As I shall try to point out very shortly,
this kind of interpretation is a gross oversimplification. The
division in the church today is between those who are loyal
to the gospel, despite their often inadequate understanding
of scriptural truth, and those committed to secular humanism, even though they may sometimes pose as representa-
tives of the church. This division crosses the lines between
clergy and laity, and it also crosses denominational lines.

Henri de Lubac, Catholic theologian, gives us this de-
scription of the crisis from a Catholic point of view:

It is clear that the Church is facing a grave crisis. Under the name of "the new Church," "the post-conciliar Church," a different Church from that of Jesus Christ is now trying to establish itself: an anthropocentric society threatened with immanentist apostasy which is allowing itself to be swept along in a movement of general abdication under the pretext of renewal, ecumenicism, or adaptation.[1]

Peter Beyerhaus, Professor of Missions at the University of Tübingen, has for some time raised his voice against the inroads of a humanistic and anthropocentric philosophy in the high places of the church. He contrasts two understandings of mission—that of "classical evangelicalism" and that of "an evolutionary theology of history."[2] The latter is making itself felt in the conciliar movement.

Catholic avant-garde theology constantly appeals to the writings of Teilhard de Chardin as presenting an alternative to classical supernaturalism. It is interesting to note that Teilhard, who died in 1955, perceived the coming church conflict: "Around us the real struggle does not take place between believers and unbelievers, but between two kinds of believers, two ideals, two concepts of God. A religion of earth is being formed against the religion of Heaven."[3] Teilhard aligns himself with the forces that oppose the old supernaturalism.

Some leading theologians noted for their social involvement nevertheless have emphasized the priority of the spiritual. I am thinking here of persons like Jacques Ellul, Thomas Merton, and Martin Luther King.[4] King declared: "I would urge you to give priority to the search for God. . . . Without God, all of our efforts turn to ashes and our sunrises into darkest nights."[5] Ellul is joined by the Catholic theologian James Hitchcock in deploring the politicalization of the gospel. Hitchcock, who is fairly liberal in his political views, calls the idea of salvation through politics "an unrecognized heresy." Ellul maintains that politics can only attain proximate objectives. It can bind the wound but cannot cure the disease.

In this connection we should also take note of Reinhold Niebuhr's warnings against utopianism and the confusion of the kingdom of God with a this-worldly paradise. Niebuhr emphasized the spiritual and transcendental character of the kingdom of God and yet saw its very concrete social relevance when rightly understood. According to him: "The Kingdom of God is not of this world; yet its light illuminates our tasks in this world and its hope saves us from despair."

Some secular theologians today are seeing the need for a renewed awareness of the transcendent in our lives. Michael Novak, a somewhat chastened secular theologian, still sees hope in political theology. Yet he says: "We require a return to the life of the Spirit. Everything else is shallow and will not heal, nor will it endure. Every effective politics is based in mysticism."[6]

Against the new theology various conservative movements have arisen in order to save the religious integrity of the church. We can mention here the No Other Gospel movement in Germany and other European countries; the Gathering about the Bible and Confessions, a high church Lutheran movement in Europe; the Good News movement in American Methodism; Presbyterians for Biblical Concerns in the United Presbyterian Church, U.S.A.; the Fellowship of Witness in the Anglican Communion; and Lutherans Alert in the American Lutheran Church. Catholic movements for conservative renewal are Catholics United for the Faith and For the Faith and the Church. Some of these new movements are reactionary both theologically and politically, but several are concerned with relating spiritual and social concern without sacrificing the former.

In opposition to a churchly conservatism, liberal and radical movements have arisen in the mainline churches with a pronounced stress on social activism. Here we can mention the Witherspoon Society in the United Presbyterian Church and the National Association of Laity in the Roman Catholic Church in America. The interdenominational Clergy and Laity Concerned also stresses radical social involvement, though it includes some who are slightly on the right of the theological spectrum. The German Protestant "Kirchentag" has increasingly come under the control of radical theologians, and though an invitation was extended to confessional evangelical leaders to participate in the 1973 Kirchentag festival, they declined on the grounds that it is now completely bereft of a biblical foundation.[7]

The Two Mentalities

Avant-garde theology reflects a new mentality, even a new religion, and it is impossible to understand the growing church conflict unless this fact is recognized. James Hitchcock makes this astute comment: "Radicals do not commonly realize that they have embraced what is in effect a new religion—the faith of radical political action, and that their new god is a jealous god who tolerates no competitors, who demands that the traditional churches be transformed to his worship and that traditional believers either convert or suffer damnation."[8]

One of the salient features of the new mentality is that salvation is understood in terms of liberation from political and economic oppression rather than release from the power of inborn sin. Indeed, politics is seen as the arena of salvation. For Dorothee Soelle, who unashamedly acknowledges the Enlightenment roots of political theology, forgiveness must be interpreted politically to mean "liberation for new life" rather than deliverance from guilt.[9] Reuben Alves argues that the new future will be realized by man in history, but with the help of God. "Salvation is achieved through a politics in which God makes man free to create" a new future for man on earth.[10] At the Eighth Ecumenical World Mission Conference in Bangkok (1973) the theme "Salvation Today" was discussed, but salvation was seen as occurring through political confrontation, and there was a call for a "moratorium" on Western missions. Salvation was equated with "the peace of the people of Viet Nam, independence in Angola, justice and reconciliation in Northern Ireland, and release from the captivity of power in the North-Atlantic Community."[11]

The main line of demarcation according to the new mentality is no longer between faith and unbelief but between political awareness and complacency in the face of social evils. The Catholic radical Rosemary Ruether refuses to draw distinctions between denominations, but she does differentiate between "those who are in the Resistance and those who are not."[12] Some of the new breed locate the gulf between men in psychological rather than political attitudes. James Pike sees the polarity in terms of the "open" versus the "uptight."

Jesus Christ is no longer the divine Savior from sin but the pattern and example of creative living. He is not the eternal Son of God incarnate in human flesh but the bearer of a religio-ethical ideal. In him we see not the condescension of the holy God but the climax of human evolution, "the maturation of the human spirit."[13] He is the prototypical faithful man who combines unfailing trust in God with unswerving loyalty to his fellowmen. He saves us by contagious love, not by a substitutionary atonement on the cross. The new salvation model is humanization rather than penal redemption. Joseph T. Nolan avers: "To propitiate an angry God is a primitivism we should have done with. Atonement suggests an outmoded explanation of redemption. . . ."[14]

While the old mentality was characterized by a provisional pessimism that viewed this world as a vale of tears, the new mentality is basically optimistic. It sees the world as implicitly Christian. Karl Rahner speaks of "anonymous Christians," those who do the good without a conscious commitment to Jesus Christ. Paul Tillich refers to the latent church which includes all those who do not belong to the manifest or visible church. The old mentality on the other hand held the devil to be the prince of the world, even though he was at the same time an unwitting instrument of the wrath and judgment of God. The new mentality lacks a solid conception of the demonic. An American Roman Catholic theologian, Henry Kelly; the Dutch theologian Piet Schoonenberg; and the Swiss Hans Haag have announced the death of Satan. It is said that the devil was a part of the cultural context in which the Bible was written rather than an essential element in the Christian faith. Pope Paul VI in reaffirming the traditional stance has stated that "the devil is enemy number one . . . who sows errors and misfortune in human history."[15]

Whereas the old mentality drew a sharp distinction between the natural and the supernatural, the new mentality virtually equates the supernatural with the natural, the sacred with the secular. Humanity and the world are thereby given divine status. Richard Wentz contends that "the world has begun to reflect the goodness of [divinity] in spite of itself."[16] Douglas Rhymes calls us to "the reverent adoration of the world" in which God seeks to bring about "the fulfillment of his purposes."[17] Against Rhymes we hold that only the Holy can be the object of ultimate concern and adoration. The secular is the realm of preliminary concerns.

In the new theology evangelism is interpreted more in terms of dialogue and consensus than of kerygmatic proclamation. Its purpose is to help men find what they already see in an imperfect way. Conversion is not so much a profound religious experience as an overcoming of social estrangement. The visual is stressed over the verbal in the communication of the gospel. It is asserted that an adequate witness can be made to the gospel without verbalizing it.

The doctrine of sin also undergoes a drastic transformation. In supposedly advanced theological circles it is no longer understood as rebellion against God but as lack of integrity and balance. Today's tragic flaws are not unbelief and idolatrous pride but sickness and ignorance. Instability is seen as a greater threat to social order than immorality. What men need, it is assumed, are therapy and enlightenment. Group therapy is especially held in high esteem, and while I am not denigrating the benefits of this kind of therapy for some people, I oppose the ideology which regards this as a panacea for the human condition.

Also given a radically new cast is the doctrine of God. While the Bible speaks of God in terms of sovereign freedom, the new theology sees God as an immanent process within the world or as a symbol for creative human interaction. It is stated that there is personality in God, but God is not as such a divine Person (Tillich). Rhymes contends that "modern thinking has cast grave doubts on the possibility of the concept of God as a separate person, whether there is any more a God out there spiritually than a God out there literally and physically."[18] Against the new thrust James Hitchcock affirms that the "Church's greatest disservice to the world would be at present to abandon its sense of God and transcendence, its accumulated spirituality, to join the world in its perplexed secularity."[19]

It should come as no surprise that prayer, too, is reinterpreted in avant-garde theology. A change in the conception of God invariably entails an alteration in the meaning and practice of prayer. In the new mentality prayer is reflection on the needs of others (Paul van Buren) or a state of radical openness (Michael Novak). It is no longer communication with a divine being but instead being in touch with oneself in a new way (Gregory Baum). Not heartfelt supplication to a merciful God, but sharing the presence of God in concern for the world—this is the hallmark of a secular understanding of prayer.

Theology is transmuted into anthropology in the new pattern of thinking. Gregory Baum has declared: "Religion is . . . man's own self-understanding and his relationship to his human and cosmic environment."[20] Bultmann and J. A. T. Robinson also see theology as essentially anthropology, the interpretation of human existence in the light of existentialist or empirical philosophy. Instead of a theology of the Word of God (as in Barth) it is now becoming customary to refer to a theology of interpersonal experience.

Authority is held to lie in the consensus of the community or in a conscience informed by the community. The infallibility of the people of God or of the general will takes precedence over an infallible Pope and an infallible Book— and an infallible Christ. In some circles an appeal is made to "the American experience" or American culture in order to construct a distinctly American theology. In other circles the ideal is a global theology that will be thoroughly cosmopolitan and that will incorporate the best insights of the world religions. A culturally enlightened humanity becomes the norm in this kind of theology. In both general approaches the city of man replaces the city of God. In much of this thinking can be detected the influence of the Enlightenment of the eighteenth century. Indeed, the new mentality is not so very new after all: instead it signifies the recrudescence of heresies that were thought to be buried in the past.

In the area of morals, situational ethics is coming to prevail over an ethics of absolute principles, at least in many of the mainline churches and seminaries. J. A. T. Robinson speaks of a morality of involvement and discovery which he contrasts with a morality of obedience. The new permissive stance is especially evident in the area of sexual ethics where anything is countenanced, even homosexual relations, so long as love is the motivating force and no one is hurt (Joseph Fletcher).[21] What the new theology does not see is that the position in which everything is permissible to man easily leads to the position that everything is permissible against man (Emmanuel Mounier). The attack on moral standards even in the name of Christian freedom begets an amorality where no values are sacred. The brutalizing pornography and indiscriminate abortion of today may well lead to the genocide of tomorrow.

In summary the new religion is utilitarian, anthropocentric, and intramundane. It has replaced a metaphysics of transcendence with a metaphysics of immanence. This stands in marked contrast to the old religion which was theocentric, centered in a transcendental vision which carried men outside of themselves toward a heavenly goal. While one strand within the new religion sees the primary goal of man as self-fulfillment and the other strand as social justice, the chief concern in biblical religion is to glorify the holy God and proclaim the coming of his kingdom.

In January, 1975, a group of concerned theologians including Peter Berger, Richard Neuhaus, Lewis Smedes, George Forell, Avery Dulles, and Alexander Schmemann gathered at Hartford, Connecticut, to draft a statement condemning certain heresies associated with secular-liberation theology and the human potential movement. What makes this conference significant is that these persons are on the whole committed to the ecumenical movement and are mainly moderate in their theological stance, though a few should be regarded as conservative. What is missing in the Hartford declaration is a clear-cut affirmation of the divine authority of Scripture, though it is an otherwise promising statement.

THE SOCIAL QUESTION

Since the new mentality emphasizes social reform and revolution as part of the essential mission of the church, those who appeal to the Bible and church tradition are confronted with the necessity to rethink the cultural mandate of the faith. Louis Evely in his *If the Church Is to Survive* (Doubleday, 1972) contends that reform has failed and that revolution is the only answer. He upholds a church in which there is no longer any distinction between the sacred and profane and in which authority is invested in the people. He favors a religious life which shuns contemplation and seeks direct involvement in all human concerns.

It is to be acknowledged that the old mentality often emphasized the spiritual perhaps to the exclusion of the secular. Yet this was its corruption, not its main thrust. Both Catholic mysticism at its best and evangelical pietism were characterized by an intense social concern which gave rise to political involvement as well as works of mercy.

Social service should be seen not as an end in itself, not as the consummation of religion, as the new mentality would have it, but as a sign and parable of the coming kingdom of God. It is ideally both a fruit of the gospel and a preparation for the gospel. If it is not viewed as a means to the uplifting and salvation of the whole man, it remains a purely worldly activity which may have value, but not a distinctly Christian value. The cultural mandate is grounded in and prepares the way for the uniquely spiritual mandate of the church (cf. 1 Cor. 10:31–33; 1 Pet. 4:11).

In my opinion the laity are in revolt not because of social stands taken by their denominations but because of the lack of moral and religious content in these social stands. They are frustrated and depressed by social preaching but not convicted. In conservative churches where a psychological emphasis preempts social concern, the layman is often soothed and tranquilized but not led into true repentance.

We need to see the social imperatives of the faith in the right perspective. Our hope lies not in a new Social Gospel but in a rediscovery of the ethical implications of the biblical gospel. The social crisis mirrors a crisis of the spirit which liberal social gospelers do not see.

In his *Righteous Empire* the distinguished church historian Martin Marty contends that the evangelical heresy which limited religion to the private, personal sphere of life accounts for the acculturization of the American church. Yet this heresy, which has also affected the liberal churches, is symptomatic of a deeper malady—the loss of faith in a transcendent, holy God. The key to the crisis in American culture is the erosion of the spiritual foundations of both social and personal religion. Private religion becomes mysticism, occultism, and psychology; social religion becomes sociology and politics. The growing chasm in the church is not between those who champion an individualistic religion and those who defend the Social Gospel but between those who hold to the biblical gospel and those who advocate secular values in the guise of culture religion.[22]

This is not to deny that many of those who pretend to speak for biblical religion are in reality proponents of culture religion. American civic religion, which appeals to many conservatives, is as much a threat as socialist democratic egalitarianism. Both types of religion are varieties of secular humanism. Liberals need to be reminded that the Word of God stands in judgment upon the counterculture as well as upon the Establishment. Conservatives need to be reminded that acquiescence in the face of social injustice blunts the impact of the gospel as much as the failure to proclaim the Word.

I concur with socially sensitive liberals that we must not remain silent or passive in the face of evil, for this only tends to reinforce evil. Biblical faith has a prophetic as well as a kerygmatic dimension. We need to rediscover the Law of God as well as the gospel if we are to have the "whole counsel of God." We must proclaim both the evangel that God declares and the righteousness that God demands (Carl Henry).

One reason why the evangelical critique of liberalism has not met with more sympathetic reaction is because many conservative critiques of social problems have themselves not been biblically anchored. The relative silence of conservative churches on the torturing of prisoners and bombing of open villages in Vietnam has served to blunt their valid questioning of the liberal call for unqualified withdrawal of American forces from Southeast Asia.[23] The attack on state paternalism when not accompanied by action to alleviate poverty in one's own community falls on deaf ears and rightly so. When theological conservatives do not speak out against such cultural right-wing shibboleths as "God helps those who help themselves," then their outcry against a growing statism will not meet with a positive response.

The horizontal dimension of love must be linked to the vertical dimension of faith. Yet the church should not try to dictate policy in government and become a competing power structure, nor should it seek from the government special privileges. The church can establish social relevance by threatening its members who participate in torture and indiscriminate killing in war with excommunication, even if they are ranking officers in the armed forces. It can also make its overall witness credible by expelling from its fold unrepentant racists, unscrupulous slum landlords, and gambling bosses. Church discipline, not clericalism, is the way to dismantle the powers and principalities.

While the old Social Gospel felt that human egoism and self-interest can be overcome by love in interpersonal relations, the new Social Gospel seeks to utilize power in bringing about social revolution. In each case the kingdom of God is identified with the "progressive" tendency in politics. I contend against both Social Gospels that political action however important pertains to the order of preservation, not redemption. With Ellul I hold that this is neither the hour for utopias nor for political realism: it is the hour for becoming aware that "Christians are so deeply imbued with the fundamental doctrines of this world that they no longer have any liberty of thought or of life."[24]

This is not to deny the right and obligation of some Christians to participate in anti-war rallies and civil-rights rallies. But their motivations and goals should be different from their worldly counterparts. The Christian will see his protest not simply as a political demonstration but as a moral convocation, a display of concern for human rights.

Evangelical Christianity is as much opposed to privatized religion as the Social Gospel, but it recognizes that new social structures, however necessary at times, are not a guarantee of justice or freedom of opportunity. The evangelical Christian sees that the "more urgent and arduous the social responsibility the greater the need for those personal resources of the spirit that enable a man to labor unceasingly without becoming . . . disheartened."[25] He will oppose and unmask the principalities and powers over against the liberals who frequently try to domesticate and humanize them. Society can finally be changed only by a revolution of the heart, and this makes the catholic evangelical position qualitatively different from the liberal position which seeks social change primarily through democratic reform. It also differentiates authentic evangelicalism from a cultural Protestant conservatism which advocates noninvolvement in the social arena and thereby the maintenance of the status quo.

NEED FOR A NEW INNER MISSION

The burning need today is for the Christianization of a secularized church. A Catholic friend active in Key 73 has declared: "We need to make living Christians out of practicing Catholics." This indeed should be the goal of the missionary outreach within the western nations: the reconversion of a nominally Christian church and culture.

The bane of the conciliar movement is that it tends to uphold the concept of an umbrella that will include as many points of view as possible. The new creed of the United Church of Christ is very acceptable as a liturgical formula, but it cannot be considered a genuine confession of faith, since even many Unitarians can subscribe to it. Pluralism may be acceptable in the penultimate sphere, but it has no place in the ultimate sphere where we are concerned with the eternal destiny of man. Modern pluralism is unfortunately rooted in a relativism that denies the validity of any claim to absolute truth. We believe that a Christian can say that he knows the truth and has the truth but not as something he controls but as something that impresses itself upon his mind and soul.

A new inner mission would seek the reform and purification of the church as well as the saving of souls. It would promote the expulsion from the church of those in high places who preach accommodation to worldly systems of thought as reflected in the death of God and the new morality. It would seek a drastic revision of Christian educational materials in many of the mainline churches which are often slanted toward secular humanism.

Behind the social malaise today is a creeping totalitarianism that takes the form of statism: this amounts to a virtual atheism, since it means giving the state the homage that belongs to God alone. It is well said that whoever rejects God becomes his brother's killer instead of his brother's keeper (Vincent Miceli). It is not enough to attack social evils; we must also recognize and unmask the spiritual malady that gives rise to these evils. Martin Luther King, unlike the advocates of violent revolution, acknowledged that men must first be "filled with God" before they can bring crucial changes to the life of society.

In our concern for the priority of the spiritual, however, we must not neglect the social dimension of the faith. We must pay heed not only to the message of the cross but also to the way of the cross. Conversion entails a change in life as well as in belief, and this involves a prophetic witness in society. Christ is Lord of all things, and the gospel must therefore be applied to all areas of life.

At the same time the church's great and primary mission is the winning of souls and the building up of Christian men and women in faith and holy living. It is imperative that we do not forget this, for basically the plight of our civilization is spiritual, not civic or social. The evangelical Christian is betraying his Lord if he does not identify himself with the struggles of the socially deprived and oppressed throughout the world, but he will be preeminently concerned with the spiritual darkness that engulfs mankind. To attend to "politics *before all else* is today to kill hope and to turn back God's gift."[26]

In addition to Christian preaching and teaching there is the hidden apostolate of prayer apart from which the great commission could never be fulfilled. Bernard of Clairvaux reminds us that evangelism "without virtues and without a deep interior life is of no value."[27] Dietrich Bonhoeffer maintains that truly Christian action can only spring from an arcane discipline of devotion. There is today need for deeper withdrawal and retrenchment if there is to be deeper penetration into the world.

In embarking on its inner mission the Christian church must avoid alliances with both the ideological right and left. Some evangelicals are attracted to the conservative political establishment, but its guiding principles are as pagan as those of the New Left. Former Vice-President Spiro Agnew has spoken of "the belief in the primacy of reason" as a hallmark of "the philosophical consensus of our nation." But the Christian church upholds the primacy of God and his sacred revelation.

The church today is torn by disunity, and this accounts in part for its lack of credibility and power. But the answer to disunity is not organic mergers based on the least common denominator. The most potent ecumenism is a spiritual ecumenism—cooperation in the great commission. Such was the emphasis of the International Congress on World Evangelization at Lausanne, Switzerland (July 1974). Our ultimate hope is, of course, for visible as well as spiritual unity. But to work for one great church that will be in effect a new world power structure is to succumb again to the secular vision. The church must resist the bid for worldly power even while maintaining a prophetic stance and concern for worldly problems.

The final hope of the Christian is for the coming of the kingdom of God and for the end of the world. Yet this hope is not to be separated from the struggle for social justice in the here and now. John Calvin recognized that "to whatever extent iniquity abounds in the world, to such an extent the kingdom of God, which brings along with it perfect righteousness is not yet come."[28] The hope of the world does not depend on worldly improvements, but it should excite us to mend the torn fabric of society. The Christian hope has a this-worldly as well as an otherworldly dimension. Because Christ is even now Lord of the world we can set up signs and parables of his past victory and his coming reign of righteousness. Rather than consigning the world to hell we should bring to the world the good news that the powers of darkness are on the run, and even though they may be making their final stand the future belongs to Jesus Christ.

NOTES

1. Quoted in Dietrich von Hildebrand, *Trojan Horse in the City of God* (Chicago: Franciscan Herald Press, 1967), p. 2. For a poignant critique of the new Catholicism from an evangelical Protestant perspective see David Wells, *Revolution in Rome* (Intervarsity, 1972).

2. Peter Beyerhaus, *Missions: Which Way?* trans. Margaret Clarkson (Grand Rapids: Zondervan, 1971).

3. Ibid., p. 86.

4. Daniel Berrigan also makes a place for the crucial role of spiritual devotion in our social action, but this is not true of a great many in the Catholic resistance movement. Berrigan's spirituality combines secular and mystical strands. What is somewhat disturbing is that his political stance closely parallels that of the New Left. Dorothy Day is another Catholic activist who more than Berrigan emphasizes the priority of the spiritual and whose piety reflects a radical faith in the gospel. While not concurring in her extreme Christ-against-culture stance, we find her witness refreshing in a time of churchly accommodation to worldly standards.

5. Martin Luther King, *Strength to Love* (New York: Harper & Row, 1963), p. 75.

6. *The National Catholic Reporter*, Vol. 9, No. 18 (March 2, 1973), p. 7.

7. See *Christianity Today*, Vol. XVII, No. 15 (April 27, 1973), p. 42.

8. James Hitchcock, *The Decline and Fall of Radical Catholicism* (New York: Herder & Herder, 1971), p. 160.

9. Dorothee Soelle, *Political Theology*, trans. John Shelley (Philadelphia: Fortress Press, 1974), p. 101.

10. Reuben Alves, *A Theology of Human Hope* (Washington, D.C.: Corpus Books, 1969), p. 144. For a similar study by a Roman Catholic scholar who conceives of theology as a rationale for social and economic liberation see Gustav Gutierrez, *A Theology of Liberation: History, Politics, and Salvation* (Orbis, 1973). Also cf. Rosemary Ruether, *Liberation Theology* (New York: Paulist Press, 1972).

11. *Christianity Today*, Vol. XVII, No. 13 (March 30, 1973), p. 17.

12. *Commonweal* (April 4, 1969), p. 66.

13. J. A. T. Robinson, *The Human Face of God* (Philadelphia: Westminster Press, 1973), p. 204. Thomas O'Meara advocates a similar stance in his *Loose in the World* (New York: Paulist Press, 1974).

14. *The National Catholic Reporter*, Vol. 9, No. 16 (February 16, 1973), p. 16.

15. *The National Catholic Reporter*, Vol. 9, No. 12 (January 19, 1973), p. 17.

16. *The Christian Century*, Vol. XC, No. 1 (January 3, 1973), p. 18.

17. Douglas Rhymes, *Prayer in the Secular City* (Philadelphia: Westminster Press, 1967), p. 43.

18. Ibid., p. 23.

19. James Hitchcock, *The Decline and Fall of Radical Catholicism*, p. 204.

20. *Commonweal* (May 15, 1970), p. 212.

21. Florence Bryant, editor of the now defunct Christian education journal *Trends* serving both the United Church of Christ and the United Presbyterians, goes so far as to propose that the church ordain gay ministers and bless "permanent and faithful" homosexual unions (July–August, 1973). Cf. Gregory Baum in *Commonweal* who calls upon Catholic homosexuals to affirm their sexual orientation in faith. Vol. XCIX, No. 19 (February 15, 1974), pp. 479–482. Also cf. Norman Pittinger who argues that the role of the Christian counselor is not to call the homosexual to change his sexual predilection but "to assist him to become a great lover." "A Theological Approach to Understanding Homosexuality" in *Religion in Life*, Vol. XLIII, No. 4 (Winter, 1974), [pp. 436–444], p. 444.

22. It is interesting to note that the liberal *Christian Century* holds to a privatistic ethic on the issue of pornography. It argues that the state should let the individual decide, that "our society is better off to leave pornography at the mercy of the adult marketplace. . . ." (July 18–25, 1973), p. 748. I commend *The Christian Century* for its bold, prophetic witness in many other areas, especially race and war.

23. While viewing as most regrettable Billy Graham's noncommittal stance on war atrocities in Southeast Asia, we applaud his stricture on apartheid in South Africa (though he was less vocal than some had hoped) and his insistence that his evange-

listic meetings in that country be open to all races. For an illuminating appraisal of what is described as "Billy Graham's inconsistent but growing social witness" see Robert G. Clouse, Robert D. Lindner and Richard Pierard, eds., *The Cross and the Flag* (Carol Stream, Ill.: Creation House, 1972), pp. 144 f.

24. Jacques Ellul, *The Presence of the Kingdom*, trans. Olive Wyon (New York: Seabury Press, 1967), p. 92.

25. Frederick Schroeder, *Visions and Renewal* (St. Louis: Eden Publishing House, 1972), p. 25.

26. Jacques Ellul, *Hope in Time of Abandonment* (New York: Seabury Press, 1973), p. 257.

27. *Collectanes Ordinis Cisterciensium Reformatorum*, XV (1953), p. 31.

28. John Calvin, *Commentary on a Harmony of the Evangelists* (Edinburgh: Calvin Translation Society, 1945), Vol. I, p. 320.

2

Burying the Gospel

When the Church becomes secular, it is the greatest con-
ceivable misfortune both for the Church and the world. And
this is what takes place when it wants to be a Church only for
the world, the nation, culture, or the state. . . . It then
loses its specific importance and meaning; the justification
for its existence.

KARL BARTH

The worst thing churchmen could do would be to lose
their nerve at the wide gap opening up between historic
Christianity and modern patterns of human behavior, and
allow themselves to be panicked by the avant-gardes into
translating the Christian message into current social mani-
festations, which are themselves part of the sickness of hu-
manity.

THOMAS TORRANCE

In their well-meaning attempts to make the gospel relevant and credible to modern man, the advocates of the new
theology have only succeeded in emptying the faith of its
biblical content. They have sought to incarnate the gospel
so fully that they have ended in burying it. They have tried
so hard to make the gospel meaningful that they have actually obscured it. By trying to make the faith this-worldly
they have secularized it. The apostles of relevance and
modernity can justly be accused of losing the identity of the

37

gospel and also of sundering continuity with the church tradition.

SOCIAL ACTIVISM

One of the hallmarks of the new mentality in the church today is the concern to establish relevance by social involvement. That the gospel has social imperatives and that Christians are under an obligation to put their faith into practice in the social arena are truths that should surely be acknowledged. Yet when social justice and material security become ends in themselves then we have lost sight of the primary goal of biblical religion which is to seek Christ's kingdom and his righteousness.

Our social action should be seen as a sign of the coming kingdom of God and as a means toward the greater glory of God. But so often in the circles of secular and political theology it becomes an end in itself or a means to the realization of a utopian dream. The gospel must not be made to serve a this-worldly utopia whether this goes under the name of the Great Society, an Opportunity State, the Classless Society, or a One World Federation of Nations. The church must never be treated as a means to political ends, for then its freedom is undermined. Political action can be accepted and encouraged as a fruit and manifestation of faith, but it becomes an effective means of burying the gospel when it is regarded as the ground or essence of faith.

Too many of our would-be prophets within the church today actually assume a pseudoprophetic stance. True prophecy is informed by Scripture and brings all sides on a controversial issue under the judgment of God. Instead of speaking the Word of God with power, many social activists unwittingly ally the faith with a social ideology be it of the radical right or the new left. When church agencies give support to African guerilla movements but are silent on the harassment of ethnic minorities in Arab Africa or black Africa (e.g., the African Christians in the Sudan, the Pygmies in Bangui and the Indians in Kenya and Uganda), then the gospel has probably been sacrificed to a cultural ideology. The merciless beating and killing of unarmed prisoners in

the African nation of Bangui by President Jean-Bedel Bo-
kassa and a detachment of his soldiers elicited no official
admonition from conciliar church bodies. President Idi Amin
of Uganda has proceeded with plans to expel from 40,000 to
50,000 Asians with only a minimal rebuke from the president
of the World Council of Churches. The savage persecution
of Jehovah's Witnesses in Malawi has evoked no measurable
protest in either liberal or conservative circles.

The recent war in Vietnam has aroused much consterna-
tion and moral indignation, and I too have voiced serious
reservations.[1] Yet some who have criticized this war have
closed their eyes to indiscriminate abortion and mercy killing, and a few have even given their tacit approval. In such
cases earnest Christians have the right to wonder whether
such political judgments spring from cultural rather than
religious values. If we as churchmen would but speak with
the authority and wisdom of prophets of the holy God, then
the world might conceivably pay heed to our admonitions.

While not disputing the right of church officials to join at
times in political demonstrations, we urge them to take care
not to identify the faith with the cause of radical leftists who
envision a society without God. When church leaders march
under the flag of the Vietcong or under such banners as
"Better Red than Dead" (as we saw in the recent past), it
is not unreasonable to ponder whether the real moral and
social imperatives of biblical faith have been disregarded.

It need hardly be said that remaining silent in the face of
controversial moral issues in society is simply another way of
burying the gospel. To explain away or rationalize any kind
of social oppression is tantamount to profaning the gospel.
The reluctance of conservatives to speak out against the
racist policies of Rhodesia and South Africa and the tendency of liberals to ignore the persecution of Christians in
Iron Curtain countries are equally deplorable. Both parties
in the church are guilty of being "selective" in their moral
indignation. Each identifies with causes that justify its ideological stance.

Revolution is now a key word in theological vocabulary,
but so often those who use it tend to support the violent
overthrow of existing social structures. This stands in con-

trast to the revolution Jesus preached, the inward transformation of the heart of man and the resultant freedom to enter into the struggle for a just society but without resort to violence. What we advocate is not less social involvement but a deeper social involvement, one that is rooted in faith in God instead of a social ideology and one that is careful never to absolutize any social program or political platform. There must be moral content in our political decisions.

Some of our larger denominations are now becoming polarized as a result of social pronouncements by ecumenical and denominational agencies which have created an attitude of suspicion and mistrust on the part of laymen. Dr. Robert Moss, president of the United Church of Christ, has declared that very little of the negative correspondence from laymen that he has received reflects serious biblical and theological study. James Gustafson, University Professor of Ethics at the Divinity School of the University of Chicago, retorts that "it is not cynical to comment that one reason for that is that most pronouncements and programs have never been given any biblical or theological justification in the first place."[2]

The resemblance between many of the social activists in the churches today and the German Christians in prewar Germany is striking. The German Christians represented various groups within the German church that sought to bring Christianity into alignment with the social and political aims of National Socialism. In the words of John S. Conway:

> They sought to rid the Church of its "pre-scientific" mentality and its archaic liturgies. . . . The essential need was not Christian orthodoxy but Christian activism, that would follow the example of the "heroic" Jesus. In place of pietistic preaching, they demanded the Church's complete commitment in political affairs. In the new creation of the Nazi Party, they saw a vehicle for their programme that offered the fellowship which they believed to be the characteristic of true Christianity.[3]

Are not these the aims also of quite a number of social revolutionaries in the churches today, except that their commitment is to democratic socialism?

PSYCHOLOGICAL ANALYSIS

The cure of souls has always played an important role in the ministry of the church. Both Luther and Calvin spoke of the need for pastoral guidance, the visitation of the sick, intercessory prayer, meditation, and private confession. In this kind of ministry the gospel was not hidden but revealed and declared; the penitent was directed to place his trust and confidence in Jesus Christ. Many of the early evangelicals advocated frequent self-examination in the light of the Word, but the Word was never subordinated to the goal of personal fulfillment.

In modern pastoral theology the therapeutic methods of secular psychotherapy figure more prominently than the spiritual direction practiced by the fathers in the faith. In the new therapy the penitent is not guided toward Christ or the Scriptures but instead is thrown back upon his own inner resources. The aim of modern nondirective counseling is rational self-understanding rather than the discovery of the will and purpose of God declared in Scripture. The emphasis is upon self-analysis and self-realization, not the greater glory of God. It is mistakenly supposed that by beginning with self one will eventually come to an understanding of God, whereas we hold with Calvin that one cannot know oneself until his eyes have been opened to the reality and majesty of God.

Many modern counselors within the church eschew any kind of overt guidance, but manipulation is present nevertheless. By the skillful use of leading questions the counselor can control the discussion and turn it toward the desired end, viz., rational insight and the resultant catharsis. Admittedly, the older form of pastoral care might also take the form of manipulation, but ideally it consisted not so much in the attempt to influence the unconscious side of the personality as in the straightforward declaration of God's mercy and an exhortation to obedience.

In sensitivity training and encounter groups the gospel is again hidden rather than proclaimed and confessed. There is direction in such groups, but it is not direction from the Word of God but from one's peers. In this kind of therapy people seek to expose their inmost feelings before others and then reexamine themselves in the light of the group reaction. The group is intended to provide support for each person, but often it assumes control sometimes in a relentlessly judgmental manner that smacks of totalitarianism. As in the older Enlightenment philosophy, it is presupposed that the truth lies within oneself and needs only to be brought out in group discussion that also entails group criticism. Not the worship and service of God but a heightened self-awareness and an awakened sense of togetherness are the goals of sensitivity training. It is hoped that by becoming more cognizant of one's own feelings one will become more open to the feelings of others. Only too often the result is a morbid preoccupation with one's self that diminishes or excludes any real interest in one's fellowman. It is interesting to note that some theological seminaries today have required courses in sensitivity training and group-dynamics but not even an elective course in prayer or devotion.

Lest I be misunderstood I do not wish to minimize the possible wholesome effects of psychological counseling and group dynamics on a certain level. The church can learn from the insights of secular psychotherapy, and one such insight is the need to listen and to cultivate empathy with the distressed person. My objection lies in the confusion of inner psychic resources with redeeming grace and the equation of catharsis and divine forgiveness. There are also grounds for criticism when nondirective counseling is substituted for spiritual direction and confession and when self-examination is regarded as the surrogate for prayer.

One can learn from secular psychotherapy, but such learning must entail discriminating between truth and error. What should be opposed is not empirical psychology but the naturalistic and humanistic philosophy that informs much of what goes under the name of psychology and also pastoral theology. The modern preoccupation with self contrasts with the biblical goal of the transcending of self in the service of God. Calvin declared: "It is His will that we should shut our eyes to what we are and have, in order that nothing may impede or even check our faith in Him." In the words of Catherine of Siena, one of the doctors of the Catholic

church: "Nothing is more His enemy than is self in me.
. . . It will be God or self, not God and self."[4] Teresa of
Avila, who was famed as a spiritual director in her time,
expressed the biblical position well when she said: "One
shall advance more by keeping eyes on divinity than keeping eyes on ourselves."[5] In our day Jacques Maritain gives
similar words of wisdom: "If we look at ourselves instead of
looking at God . . . we wander disquieted instead of entering into peace." The paradox of the Christian faith was
cogently expressed by our Lord when he said that by losing
ourselves in the service of the kingdom of God we shall find
ourselves, but when we seek to find or discover ourselves
then we shall lose ourselves (Luke 9:24, 25; John 12:25).

Our plea is not for less pastoral care but for one that is
anchored in the wisdom of Scripture and the catholic tradition. We need to listen and be nondirective at times in our
counseling, but we must always seek finally to bring the gospel into the open and not let it remain hidden. Dr. George
Benson, a Christian psychiatrist and psychoanalyst, has said
that "today people will not be led to change save by one
who speaks with priestly authority."[6]

Too often the church today seeks to promote fellowship
by group techniques instead of letting fellowship spontane-
ously arise by giving its people a vision and higher purpose
in life. I agree with the admonition of Mary Shideler: "The
fashion of promoting 'fellowship' as such is foredoomed because authentically personal relationships cannot be manipu-
lated by direct techniques." She goes on to say that they are
usually the by-products of something else, such as, shared
work.[7] True fellowship arises when people are gripped by
the passion of faith and are moved to give of themselves for
the cause of the gospel.

When the gospel is given explicit recognition by pastoral
psychologists, it is often treated as a means to an end, viz.,
the fulfillment and happiness of the individual. But the gospel cannot be made into a tool for solving man's problems
nor can it be used as a stepping stone to man's personal
growth. We must also affirm that the gospel does not guarantee happiness and security for the believer. Indeed, if we
are true to Scripture, we discover that the gospel brings new

problems and that it promises not happiness as the world understands it but instead the cross of affliction and suffering (cf. Matt. 10:34–39).

This is not to overlook those in the fields of psychology and psychiatry who are seeking to do justice to the spiritual dimension, such as Paul Tournier, O. Quentin Hyder, and Bernard Martin. Nor is it to disregard those in the area of pastoral theology who have in varying degrees remained true to the evangelical and catholic tradition of pastoral care, such as Arvid Runestam, Canon E. N. Ducker, Eduard Thurneysen, and Jay Adams.[8] But the danger of psychologism, that is, the idea that psychological analysis supplies the key to the fathoming of the human spirit, is very real in all these circles, and the church must be alive to this ever present temptation.

LITURGICAL INNOVATION

The new liturgy, like the new theology which informs it, also tends to bury instead of exalt the gospel. New liturgical experiments that feature agape meals, guitar masses, audio-visual aids, and religious drama often leave out the one thing that is most important as far as evangelical theology is concerned—the preaching and hearing of the Word of God. The heart of the gospel, say the avant-garde liturgists, is not a rational message but an experience of community or a style of life. The Catholic lay theologian Leslie Dewart contends in his *The Future of Belief* that Christianity has a *"mission, not a message. . . .* What it communicates is its reality and existence, not an idea."

In contradistinction to the liturgical tradition the new style liturgy is centered not in God's revelation but in man's faith. It is geared to the celebration of the festivity of life instead of the Word made flesh. Its concern is with the search for identity rather than the worship of a living, personal God. At the Ninth Youth Quadrennial of the Presbyterian Church U.S. in Atlanta several years ago one of the worship leaders gave this definition of liturgy: "Liturgy is something which relates me to my neighbor, which makes me feel good, which gives me identity." At a jazz mass broadcast over television from St. Mark's Episcopal Church in New York City one of the celebrants remarked: "Our aim is to help people to feel something—anything." James Colaianni, the former lay secretary of the Liturgical Conference in the Roman Catholic Church, states that "the entire meaning of liturgy" can be summed up in the word "empathy" and "worship is a word religion should try to forget."[9] Jesus is upheld as a court jester (Cox) or a social revolutionary rather than the Savior from sin. A this-worldly optimism pervades the new liturgism. The pleasures and vitalities of life are given prominence whereas the Bible speaks of joy amid suffering. In the view of Harvey Cox erotic dancing, intoxicating drinks and drugs can all have a place in a "festive liturgy."[10]

Another characteristic of the new liturgism is the loss of the moral imperatives of the faith. Despite the fact that many of the new liturgies are focused upon the critical social issues of the day, such as peace, race, and poverty, the theology that is presented undermines effective social action for it disallows any kind of moral discrimination. Kent Schneider, a liturgical jazz artist, declares: "When we say celebrate, we mean that we celebrate the entire world, not just those things that we like, but all the good and evil aspects of life that feed into our consciousness."[11] The Ecumenical Institute in Chicago, which has pioneered in liturgical experimentation, has for its slogan, "All that is, is good." In the theology of this community everyone is "totally accepted," "everything is approved." No wonder that in its advocacy of social revolution any means is countenanced for the realization of a new society.

Liturgical innovations are also evident in "ecumenical happenings" which bring together Catholics and Protestants and very often Jews, Moslems, and nonbelievers as well. A great many of these "ecumenical" services are characterized by syncretism and latitudinarianism. The "sermon" is usually focused upon social betterment or social-personal integration rather than upon the gospel, and this is not surprising since the service in order to attract must be based upon what the various participants have in common. At an ecumenical Eucharist service in Cumberland, Rhode Island, a Hindu swami took part in the celebration apparently without any objection being raised.

In 1970 an ecumenical group of Bostonians, which included Harvey Cox, held a "Mass" on the Eastern Orthodox Easter, incorporating elements from both Roman Catholic and Orthodox liturgies. But its purpose apparently was not to bear witness to the historical resurrection of Christ but to celebrate life, peace, and human brotherhood. Here we see how traditional symbols are utilized for essentially secular festivals and are thereby emptied of their original content.

Liturgical experimentation can be wholesome so long as it is informed by Scripture and by the wisdom of the church tradition. I oppose the reactionaries who merely wish to restore liturgical patterns of a bygone day just as I criticize the new liturgism that derives its inspiration from contemporary secular fads. What is needed is a new kind of liturgy but one that stands in continuity with the past and is centered about the Word and the sacraments. Helmut Thielicke in his *The Trouble with the Church* has said that the two main threats to the church today are the liturgiologists and the musicologists because of their penchant toward archaism. He was speaking before the rise of the new liturgism that buries the gospel in contemporaneity. As evangelicals we should seek neither to ape Catholic practices nor simply repristinate the cultus of the Reformation churches; instead we should boldly create new forms of faith rooted in the past but relevant to the present.

CULTURAL PREACHING

Although preaching is indispensable for full Christian worship, it is nevertheless true that much if not most preaching today buries the gospel in abstraction and triviality and our people are consequently not being spiritually fed. What they are hearing from the pulpits today is not biblical, evangelical preaching but random thoughts on a cultural or ideological theme. This is preaching that reflects and undergirds the biases of the community, that soothes rather than challenges, diverts rather than convicts.

Cultural preaching is often characterized by a false irenicism, since an attempt is made to please all factions. The pastor gives compromise solutions instead of forthrightly declaring the biblical word of truth that brings all sides under judgment. He deludes himself into thinking that he is an agent of reconciliation while in reality his preaching has the effect of reconciling no one, though people may be brought into outward agreement. In biblical eyes, heartfelt repentance is the prerequisite for reconciliation, and repentance entails the confession of sin against God as well as against neighbor.

Those who uphold a new Social Gospel are often cultural preachers because they unite the gospel with the ideology of the New Left and thereby substitute propaganda for proclamation. Instead of trying to discover the social implications of the biblical gospel, they bring to their flocks a new gospel concerning a kingdom of man that can be realized by social engineering. The ambassador of Christ must never preach social action, but he should proclaim God's law and relate it to the social condition, and when he does this his congregation is then ready to hear the gospel, the good news of God's mercy revealed in Jesus Christ. Too many preachers are commentators on society and not genuine prophets who bring the Word of God to bear upon the cultural crisis of our time.

Sectarian preaching is another way of hiding the light of the gospel by enthroning the wisdom of men. What is proclaimed is not the whole gospel but a segment of the gospel, not the biblical evangel but the pet doctrines of the denomination. The sectarian preacher parrots the party line of his church and thereby confuses the infallible truth of God with the fallible truths of men. When the extraordinary gifts of the Spirit or biblical prophecy or the divine decrees of predestination become the sole or even the primary content of our message, then we have betrayed the biblical mandate to preach the gospel and teach men to be disciples of Jesus Christ.

What Peter Forsyth terms "impressionistic preaching" also obscures the gospel, since the purpose here is not to uphold the Word of God but to impress people with one's own erudition and accomplishments. Such preachers may be excellent

speakers and even capable scholars, but they are not spokesmen for God. They are burying the gospel in order to win
the admiration of men and thereby advance themselves in
the church and also in the world.

The gospel fares little better in what has come to be
known as "dialogic preaching" which usually involves not
an exposition of Scripture but an exchange of opinions. The
preacher and his congregation together declare themselves
willing to search for the truth but sedulously avoid standing
under the judgment of the truth already declared in Jesus
Christ. There is a place for dialogue between preacher and
congregation but on the basis of the sermon preached and
the Scripture read. Philip Spener argued for Sunday evening
meetings in which the people could discuss the theme of the
morning sermon, but the discussion would be in the light of
Scripture, the infallible rule for all faith and practice.

Church Mergers

The trend toward church mergers outwardly appears a
good thing, since it was our Lord's will that his people be
one (cf. John 17:20–23). Biblical faith does not rest content
with spiritual unity, however necessary that is, but presses on
to give visible, concrete expression to our unity in Christ.

At the same time visible unity is contingent upon a common understanding of the truth of faith, and when truth is
sacrificed for organizational union the gospel is again
eclipsed. Dietrich Bonhoeffer warned against this danger in
his criticism of the ecumenical movement: "The Churches
in the World Alliance have no common recognition of the
truth. . . . We may not play with the truth, or else it will
destroy us."[12] In Bonhoeffer's view seeking to come to terms
with the hard facts of doctrinal differences cannot be
avoided if true unity is ever to be an accomplished fact.
Conciliar theologians, however, frequently brush aside doctrinal barriers and attempt to forge a visible unity on the
basis of common social goals (secular ecumenism). Altar
and pulpit fellowship between the churches in my estimation is not dependent on a doctrinal consensus on all matters,

but it does presuppose a basic concord concerning the fundamentals of the faith.

In a significant address at the Aquinas Institute of Theology in Dubuque, Iowa (September 28, 1973), Greek Orthodox Archbishop Iakovos voiced his concern that the World Council of Churches is being deflected from its spiritual aims by a social involvement that lacks biblical and theological grounding.[13] In his mind the conciliar movement now appears to operate under a double standard which advocates a hands-off policy on Northern Ireland and the Iron Curtain nations but total involvement in the struggles of the Third World even to the extent of supporting violent insurrection. Warning that the Council was no longer abiding by scriptural principles in its social and political actions, he called for a renewal of its commitment to the cause of Christian unity. Such commitment entails theological dialogue at the deepest level animated by a concern for scriptural truth and a love for the brethren. In his eyes the key to Christian unity does not lie in forging a new political ideology but in a rediscovery of the imperatives of Scripture and a rededication to the Lordship of Jesus Christ.

Another disquieting note in ecumenical relations today is that in many quarters the motivation for church union does not seem to be a united witness before the world but greater efficiency in organization. There is indeed cause for concern if a new kind of denominational imperialism is being substituted for the spreading of the good news and the advancement of the kingdom of God. Some ecumenists envision a super-church characterized by a common polity and a unified liturgy, but this contradicts the New Testament vision of the church where there is liturgical diversity and various forms of ministry but at the same time a common devotion to the faith once delivered to the saints. The church in the present age of crisis and revolution must not seek to preserve itself by organizational solidification but must be willing to die for the sake of the gospel. The choice that lies before the church today is to bury the gospel in organizational bureaucracy and high-powered public relations or to strip down its program for institutional survival so that more energy can be given to the task of evangelism and mission.

Despite the continued advance of ecumenism there is probably more disunity in the churches today than has been the case since the period of the Reformation. Organizational consolidation has only served to aggravate the tensions and divisions in the church caused by the general departure from biblical moorings and the politicalizing and psychologizing of religion. It is my conviction that before there can be authentic unity there must first be a genuine spiritual awakening in which people will be confronted by the gospel and challenged to decision.

CRISIS IN THE CHURCH

The shadow of schism lies over the modern church, both Catholic and Protestant, as the polarization between conservatism and liberalism deepens. Many churches and theologians today are trying to substitute consensus for polarization, but this is seeking unity at the expense of truth. The ground for reconciliation is God's saving act in Christ and not common cultural interests or institutional survival.

It is well to note that the New Testament urges us to avoid not polarization but factionalism and party spirit. The gospel indeed creates a new polarization between belief and unbelief. The gospel is folly to those who are perishing (1 Cor. 1:18), and wherever it is proclaimed men will be confronted with the scandal of the cross that will necessarily cause offense. The church will be plotting a suicidal course if it seeks to hide this offense by a dubious apologetics. The way to end polarization is by conversion and submission to Jesus Christ, the Lord of the church.

Liberal theologians never tire of asserting that the crisis today is one of ethical obedience. That the people of God are not obeying his will in the present situation cannot be gainsaid, but behind this disobedience is the deeper crisis of faith. One cannot do the truth unless he is in the truth, and therefore the trumpet of the modern church gives an uncertain sound (cf. 1 Cor. 14:8). Many churches and seminaries today have become fields for evangelism rather than forces of evangelism, and this means that apostasy is rife even

among the sons of the kingdom. It is well to recognize that
unbelief is constantly pictured in the Old Testament as an
even more heinous sin than social injustice. The church has
been addressing itself to symptoms and has been ignoring
the roots of the cancer that afflicts modern society.

New idolatries are emerging to fill the spiritual vacuum
created by the reluctance of the church to let the truth of the
gospel shine into the hearts of men. Among these new ob-
jects of deification are the group mind or the social consciousness (as in groupism and progressive education); the nation
or race (as in the new nationalism and militarism); the social
class (as in Marxism); and the vital instincts (as in pansexu-
alism). The church today is challenged to unmask these
pseudogods, but it is greatly hampered in this task by its
subservience to ideology, whether this be of the right or the
left.

Hand in hand with the new idolatries has arisen a new
morality which is openly skeptical of any moral absolute and
which for all practical purposes serves the technological
revolution. The Watergate scandal is a recent expression of
this morality. Its aim is adjustment to the cultural norm, and
its high priests are the social scientists and psychologists.
Jacques Ellul is one theologian and social analyst who has
been alert to the encroaching danger of a "technological
morality" which, in his words, "appears as a suppression of
morality through the total absorption of the individual into
the group."[14]

A new "democratic" totalitarianism has emerged that
seeks to enlist the aid of both the right and the left. Those
who give their allegiance to "the rights of man" in the abstract instead of the glory of God and whose slogan is "All
power to the people" are unwittingly preparing the way for
a totalitarian take-over. They give lip service to the democratic ideal but in reality the society they envision would be
tightly controlled by an oligarchy of sociologists, educators, and psychologists.

The church can only cope with the present crisis if it becomes ever more sensitive to social reality by freeing itself
from its bondage to ideology. Instead of trying to come to
terms with the growing unbelief in our times it should seek

to unmask it as well as proclaim the faith in all of its purity and power. It should also be alive to apostasy from within and, particularly, to the secular humanism that has infiltrated the new Social Gospel movement. This kind of humanism is also present in the conciliar movement as well as in the circles of religious education and pastoral theology. For the sake of true ecumenism and an authentically Christian education, church theologians should begin applying themselves to the task of the defense of the faith within the church.

What is needed today is a new kind of dogmatics that will at the same time be an apologetics, one that will not hide nor embellish the gospel but confront the world with the gospel. It would be an apologetics in the service of a kerygmatic theology. It would not seek to make the gospel credible or plausible to the world, but it would not hesitate to expose the pitiful delusions of a great many moderns and the emptiness of their own philosophies in the face of the world crisis.

Martin Marty, rightly I believe, maintains that we are entering an apocalyptic age, an age when the certainties of yesterday will probably be taken from us. The often shallow optimism that has permeated secular and political theology will prove insufficient to cope with the harsh realities that lie ahead. Instead of an optimism based on the inherent perfectibility of man and evolutionary progress, the world stands in need of an optimism founded on the divine realities of justification and regeneration. The death of God will be followed by the death of the church unless the church abandons the gods of popular culture-religion and begins listening again to the voice of the true God as it is found in Holy Scripture. Then it might rediscover its true role and mission which is to uphold the glorious gospel of redemption before a lost and despairing world and thereby to prepare the way for the coming kingdom of God.

NOTES

1. I condemned the war in Indo-China several years ago in an article entitled "This Immoral War" (1968) which was circulated at the Republican State Convention in Iowa.

2. In *The Chicago Theological Seminary Register*, Vol. LXI, No. 4 (May, 1971), p. 6.

3. John S. Conway, *The Nazi Persecution of the Churches 1933–45* (New York: Basic Books, 1968), p. 11.

4. Quoted in Albert Day, *An Autobiography of Prayer* (New York: Harper & Bros., 1952), p. 169.

5. Ibid., p. 107.

6. See George Benson, "The Disavowal of Priestly Authority" in *The Christian Century*, Vol. LXXXVI, No. 22 (May 28, 1969), [pp. 739–741], p. 740.

7. In her *Consciousness of Battle* (Grand Rapids: Wm. B. Eerdmans, 1970), p. 106.

8. See especially Jay Adams, *Competent to Counsel* (Nutley, N. J.: Presbyterian & Reformed, 1971). Also cf. his *The Christian Counselor's Manual* (Presbyterian and Reformed, 1973).

9. In James Hitchcock, *The Decline and Fall of Radical Catholicism*, p. 59.

10. See Harvey Cox, *The Feast of Fools* (Cambridge: Harvard University Press, 1969).

11. *United Church Herald*, Vol. 12, No. 11 (Nov., 1969), p. 16.

12. Dietrich Bonhoeffer, *No Rusty Swords*, trans. Edwin Robertson and John Bowden (New York: Harper & Row, 1965), p. 172.

13. It should be noted that Archbishop Iakovos has been active in the civil rights movement and has established a reputation as a "bold" leader in a branch of Christendom that has often encouraged mystical detachment from the world.

14. Jacques Ellul, *To Will & To Do* (Philadelphia: Pilgrim Press, 1969), p. 168.

3

The Church

and Social Involvement

The Churches have proved to be lamentable ambassadors and have failed to play their revolutionary part. Instead of acting as a ferment or a leaven in society, too often they have either been immersed in the lowest form of politics, or in a "spirituality" which has lost touch with ordinary life.

JACQUES ELLUL

As has been indicated earlier, the running debate in the church today concerns the role of social involvement in its wider mission. The growing disenchantment of many church people with the National and World Council of Churches can be explained in part as a reaction to the pronouncements of those organizations on a great number of critical social issues.

It is my contention that the church has a spiritual mission in a temporal context. The Christian ideal is the spiritual *in* the secular, the spiritual related to the concrete concerns and issues of life. Our duty is not to withdraw or detach ourselves from the world but to advance the kingdom of God in the world. We do this directly by spiritual means, including the Word and sacraments and the life of devotion. But we can also do this indirectly, and here temporal means may be employed. Laws are needful to restrain the powers of the

55

old aeon, even though such laws have only a negative role in the spreading of the gospel.

Luther's motto was "faith active in love," and though I share this ideal, I believe that it must be supplemented by "love seeking justice" (William Lazareth). The church has a prophetic as well as an evangelical ministry. This is to say it must bring the Law of God to bear upon the social order. It must be the critic and moral monitor of the world. Evangelical indicatives must be combined with moral imperatives.

The purpose of the Law is spiritual. It is to uphold before men the commandments of God thereby convicting them of sin and driving them to the gospel. It also is to give men the standards upon which they can pattern their lives. When we preach the Law we should always seek to relate it to the gospel, for it is the gospel that creates the new man.

Conservative Protestants have generally emphasized the need for the personal appropriation of the gospel by politicians and statesmen rather than the social demands of the Law upon politics and the state. But an obedient church will be involved in both kinds of activity. In addition to heralding the gospel call to conversion it will preach the Law of God in its social dimensions.

Yet the social involvement of the church as a church will be indirect. The church becomes involved socially by means of its proclamation of the Word of God in the form of the Law. It is not the task of the church to offer a blueprint for a new society or propose specific solutions to social problems. Instead its duty is to arouse the conscience of society by its proclamation. It is incumbent upon the church to preach the Law, the state to apply the Law. Christian laymen upon hearing the Law will be moved by conviction of sin to redress social wrongs and abuses. Prophetic criticism can be given by the church directly. Social action should be carried out by individual Christians in the world.

This is not to deny that Christian laymen may at times act corporately in facilitating social justice, but they will be acting in their role as concerned citizens and in conjunction with other concerned people. There may indeed be occasions when they would wish to bring a distinctly Christian witness to bear on the social situation, and here the lines between the cultural and spiritual mandates of the church may become somewhat hazy. Yet the church best maintains its identity and integrity when it holds fast to the principle that the two mandates are not the same, even though the distinctions may not always be clear in actual practice.

The church has both a prophetic and priestly function. Its prophetic role is fulfilled when it calls society to account for its misdeeds before the bar of God's judgment. But the church is called to speak to *moral* issues; it should not become embroiled in patently ideological disputes. The pastor-prophet will go to the heart of the problem, to the moral principle involved. The church exercises its priestly function when it guides Christians in their social action toward fruits that are in keeping with repentance and faith.

We as Christians cannot convert social structures nor can we Christianize politics. But we can reform social structures in the light of God's Law. We can also humanize politics with the Law and gospel as our criteria. We cannot build a utopian society, but we can help to move society toward a higher degree of justice through our prophetic criticism and social action.

One danger that the church should beware of is clericalism. Here the church not only preaches the Law but seeks to "aid" the state in enforcing the Law thereby becoming a power structure within the society. The opposite peril is ghettoism in which the church detaches itself from the burning social issues of the time. The church should not seek to impose its will on the state nor should it try to control the state. But it can admonish the state when the state attempts to usurp powers that belong only to God. It can also provide the state with spiritual principles that inform and direct a social program. The political world is not autonomous and therefore is not immune to the prophetic criticism of the church. The church should be neither the master nor the servant of the state but its conscience (Martin Luther King). It should be the goad that reminds the state of its guilt and powerlessness before God.

Though the church must relate itself to the critical issues in society in its proclamation of the Law, its chief concern is with the divine plan of salvation. It is well to bear in mind

that the church is not a political forum nor a social welfare
agency nor a counseling center: it is essentially a mission
enterprise. Its primary task is to spread the gospel and convert souls. Yet it should encourage its members to enter
politics and social work and bring to them a Christian orientation. Government work as such is secular work, but we are
called to live in the secular even while having a spiritual
purpose and direction.

Instead of stating the case for a Christian politics we
should point to the need for the Christian in politics. The
Christian by virtue of his higher calling is always obligated
to rise above partisan politics. He will never fit into a political mold. He will forever be a thorn in the flesh to those who
are committed to an ideological position. The Christian
works in politics for a spiritual end—to call the attention of
men to the claims of Jesus Christ. Only when he has this
spiritual purpose does his political or social work become
kingdom service.

Jacques Ellul, a French Reformed layman active in politics, reminds us of the limitations and motivations of the
Christian's social involvement: "He must plunge into social
and political problems in order to have an influence on the
world, not in the hope of making it a paradise, but simply in
order to make it tolerable—not in order to diminish the opposition between this world and the Kingdom of God, but
simply in order to modify the opposition between the disorder of this world and the order or preservation that God
wills for it—not in order to 'bring in' the Kingdom of God,
but in order that the Gospel may be proclaimed, that all men
may *really* hear the good news of salvation, through the
Death and Resurrection of Christ."[1]

Christians should be encouraged to join others who are
sensitive to social evils in order to bring a higher degree of
justice to the world. We can cooperate with others because
of the universal moral law written in conscience and also
because of our common involvement in sin. We should see
our fellow-workers in politics more as aroused fellow-sinners
than as men of good will. Like ourselves they have mixed
motivations, but they are undoubtedly moved in their concern for justice out of an uneasy conscience. While the non-

Christian generally seeks human survival and a fair deal for himself and the group with which he identifies, the Christian seeks a justice that is informed by selfless love. The secular conception of justice is giving each man his due; the biblical understanding of justice is to bring people into a right relationship with one another. It both fulfills and transcends the secular conception.

CHURCH AND STATE

In order to understand more fully the prophetic role of the church in society it is well to recall to mind that there are in the biblical view two jurisdictions—the spiritual and the temporal. These should not be divorced, for the temporal must always be informed by the spiritual. Just as reason should be illumined by faith so justice should be enlightened by love.

When the Pharisees inquired of Jesus whether it was lawful to pay taxes to Caesar, Jesus took a coin and asked them whose inscription it bore. When they acknowledged that it carried the inscription of Caesar, our Lord said: "Render therefore to Caesar the things that are Caesar's and to God the things that are God's." (Matt. 22:15–22; Luke 20:19–26). This statement has frequently been misinterpreted to imply that there are areas in life that are exempt from God's rule. But Jesus was not pointing to two kingdoms that stand over against one another and that are therefore equally legitimate. Instead he was reminding his hearers that we live under two authorities: one is absolute or ultimate, and the other is relative, provisional, and derivative. All things belong to God, but tribute may be given to Caesar who is the temporary custodian of what is first of all God's. Helmut Thielicke contends that Matthew 22:21 points to both the divine empowering and the divine relativizing of Caesar. "Bound to God, we are free both for Caesar and from Caesar."[2]

It is well to note that Luther spoke in this connection of two governments (*Regimenten*), not two kingdoms (*Reichen*), showing that we are dealing not with two spheres but with two modes of the divine rule. Yet Luther mainly

saw the state as a "dyke against sin," belonging to the order
of preservation. Calvin saw the state in a more positive
light, as a means by which men show their calling to lives of
servanthood. Likewise the Law for Calvin has more than a
negative, restraining function: it can also guide men in their
secular vocations. Both of these Reformers also affirmed the
reality of the two kingdoms, that of God and the devil, light
and darkness, good and evil; the kingdom of evil may indeed
penetrate the church as well as the state.

It is clear in the total context of Jesus' teaching that he
forbids homage to Caesar. It is well to remember that tem-
ples to Caesar were being set up in the Roman Empire, but
these were viewed by the apostolic church as centers of
iniquity and idolatry. It can be said that our Lord affirms
secularity, which is rendering to Caesar the things that are
Caesar's. But he opposes secularism, which is rendering to
Caesar the things that are God's.

While the chief task of the state is to insure social justice
and order, the primary task of the church is to turn men to
God. The Bible tends to speak of two orders—redemption
and preservation. It also affirms the principle of the two
swords—the Word of God and political coercion. The church
is under the divine mandate to wield the first sword and the
state the second (cf. Rom. 13:4). The Bible affirms both the
Law "which worketh wrath" (Rom. 4:15, KJV) and the "faith
which worketh by love" (Gal. 5:6, KJV). Here we also see
Christ's strange work, that of judgment, and his proper work,
that of salvation. While the state is the agent of Christ's
strange work, the church is the instrument of his proper
work. To be sure, the church, too, can be an agent of God's
wrath through the Word that it proclaims, but it must never
seek to be a political instrument of his wrath. Individual
Christians likewise should not try to be agents of God's
vengeance, but they must be willing to be so especially if
their office or position in society requires it.

The church ideally will recognize the divine sanction of
the state. It will acknowledge that God rules through the
state although in a different way from his rule through the
church. The church should see that it has a different juris-

diction and responsibility from that of the state, but it may call the state to live up to its own mandate. The church should be socially conscious but not politically aligned.

Yet churchmen should also recognize the demonic temptations that confront the state and also the church. The church must always insist on the freedom to proclaim and serve the Word of God. When this freedom is endangered by the state, then the church is placed in opposition to the political powers.

Bonhoeffer maintained that the church can act in three possible ways toward the state. It can first of all ask the state whether its actions are "legitimate and in accordance with the state." Secondly, it can aid the victims of the state. Finally, it can act in defiance of the state. "The third possibility," he wrote in 1932, "is not just to bandage victims under the wheel, but to put a spoke in the wheel itself."[3] Yet in his view open defiance of the state should be considered only as a last resort when no other means are available to the church.

In the Old Testament we have many examples of these various ways of relating to the state. The prophets, including Isaiah, Jeremiah, Amos, and Micah, constantly reproved the nation of Israel for not abiding by the divine commandment. They were giving prophetic criticism of the state in the light of God's Word. An example of aid to victims of the state is to be found in 1 Kings 18 where Obadiah, the comptroller of the household of Ahab, hid one hundred prophets in caves to protect them from Jezebel's interdict. He was willing to take this risk because he was a "devout worshiper of the Lord." David's open defiance of Saul and Jeremiah's counsel to Zedekiah to surrender are illustrations of treasonable activities which place the man of God in direct opposition to the policies of the state.

Helmut Thielicke contends in his *Theological Ethics* Vol. II that it is never the church's task to recommend particular political solutions nor to undertake revolutionary activity or initiate active resistance to the state, though individual Christians may do so. The task of the church is instead to be a "watchman," exposing and clarifying moral issues in politics, trying to reconcile men with one another. It should also passively resist anti-Christian laws and state denials of human freedom.

In his provocative book, *Who Speaks for the Church?* Paul Ramsey chides the World Council of Churches for proposing political solutions to social problems and thereby seeming to usurp the prerogatives of the state.[4] In his view the church should point directions but not issue directives. Its task is to be a moral guide. It should endeavor to shape the moral ethos but not dictate policy.

While basically in sympathy with Ramsey, I believe that on occasion the church is compelled to issue directives, for the Word of God takes on concreteness in this way. On the question of Vietnam it was incumbent upon the church to raise its voice against the torturing of prisoners and the bombing of open villages, but when some of its spokesmen urged the state to withdraw our forces unilaterally from Vietnam or support a neutralist or Communist government for South Vietnam, then the church was no longer abiding by its spiritual mandate.

Ramsey sometimes implies that church councils cannot speak for the church when there is no broad consensus in the church. But then there would be no prophetic speaking at all, since the prophetic word will invariably go counter to the thinking of the community at large. It should also be recognized that consensus in a church council is no guarantee that men have really discerned the will of God. The true prophet will often have to stand alone, speaking out against the councils of the church as well as against popular feeling.

Reinhold Niebuhr, who is noted for his realistic approach to social issues, has also voiced misgivings on the readiness of church bodies to offer specific solutions to social ills. He declares:

> A part of the Church . . . has been ready to elaborate detailed schemes of justice and of law for the regulation of the political and social life of mankind, below the level of love and of grace. But it has involved itself in a graceless and inflexible legalism. It does not know that all law can easily be the instrument of sin; that inflexible propositions of justice . . . may hinder rather than help the achievement of true justice.[5]

The church should never try to convert the state into another church. The church should be the church and proclaim the Word of God, and the state should be the state, enforcing justice and maintaining order. The church points men to the spiritual righteousness of the kingdom while the state concerns itself with civil righteousness, which sustains but does not redeem men.

Concerning the polity of the state, democracy is preferable to theocracy because of the misuse of power by sinful men. The best government is one which maintains checks and balances against the abuse of power. Mass or popular democracy in which the voice of the people is identified with the voice of God is a threat to the church because it signifies another kind of idolatry. A Christian democracy or a Christian political party can present problems because such a venture may tie the church to a social ideology and actually impede its prophetic witness. The church as a church should seldom if ever promote political parties that seek to implement "Christian" principles; yet Christian laymen might lend their support to such enterprises under exceptional circumstances. The polity that seeks a balance of power and a fair representation for conflicting interests is best not only for the state but also for the church.[6]

It should be remembered that the kingdom of God is not a democracy but an absolute monarchy. The truth of the gospel must never be subject to confirmation or ratification by the people, but the word of the pastor must, of course, be subjected to scrutiny under the Word of God. This applies even more to church bureaucrats and educators who often function as elitist groups exempt from criticism. The prophetic voice does not usually arise out of a committee unless someone has a Bible.

The church should remind the state that there is a law higher than the civil law and a power higher than the temporal power. It should bring the law of God to bear on specific actions of the secular community particularly where moral behavior is concerned.

William Lazareth rightly points out that the church can speak authoritatively for God but must not presume that it can speak infallibly as God.[7] Otherwise it too becomes susceptible to the penetration of the prince of darkness. It must, of course, be acknowledged that infallible truth can be conveyed by the church, but the church must never make the claim that its judgments are a priori free from error, that is, infallible in principle.

The church is the custodian of the Law as well as the servant and herald of the gospel; it therefore has a twofold ministry. When it exercises this twofold ministry, its message becomes both socially relevant and evangelically profound. The church is not called to solve the problems of society, but it is obliged to relate to them and challenge them, and it does this in its proclamation of the Law.

DUAL CITIZENSHIP

The Christian has a dual citizenship. He is a citizen of the secular state and also a member of the kingdom of heaven. He is generally born into the first but always adopted into the second. He lives in two aeons—the temporal and the spiritual. He must seek justice in the old aeon even while his hope is in the righteousness of the kingdom that is still to come as a universal reality.

The goal of the Christian is to be the best citizen of two worlds. What disturbs me about the new theology is that it presupposes that there is only one world, and this means that the Christian is under only one obligation—to seek his own temporal welfare and that of others. In my view the Christian has a dual responsibility. As a citizen of the state, he is obliged to work for social justice. But as a citizen of the kingdom of heaven, it is incumbent upon him to call men to that higher righteousness—life with God in eternity.

It is well to note that the laws of the kingdom of God are not and cannot be the same as the laws of the secular order. Jesus' command to his disciples that they offer no resistance to one who is evil (Matt. 5:39) cannot be made to apply to the secular realm, for then society would be threatened with chaos. How we act as an ambassador of Christ will often be different from how we act as a responsible citizen of the state. A judge is not fulfilling his responsibility as a citizen in a governmental office if he refuses to sentence a willful transgressor of the civil law to prison. On the other hand, when he brings the prisoner a cup of cold water in the spirit of Christian love, he is fulfilling his obligations as a member of the kingdom. His responsibility in the public domain will thus vary from his duties in the personal or private sphere of life, and yet the two are integrally related just as the Law and gospel are related.

This may sound very Lutheran, but Luther's view on these questions has much to commend it; indeed, it can be shown to be biblically grounded. Luther's position, which holds Christ and culture in paradox, needs to be supplemented by Calvin's conversionist stance, which depicts Christ as the transformer of culture;[8] yet both reformers stoutly adhered to the concept of the two governments and ipso facto to the dual citizenship of the Christian. I am not advocating a rigid dualism, for the secular goal should always be informed and judged by the spiritual goal. Indeed, it should be seen as a means to the spiritual goal. Returning to the illustration, the judge should see the prison sentence that he metes out as an opportunity to bring the transgressor to repentance. What we are affirming is that the Christian has two modes of responsibility, and these must not be confused lest society fall into disorder.

Though the church, as such, belongs wholly to the new aeon, it must address itself to the misdeeds, fears, and agonies of the old aeon. Yet when it does so, its overall purpose should always be to prepare men for membership in a kingdom that is spiritual and invisible (Luther), a kingdom that is not of this world. Its social involvement and social action should be regarded as a means to a higher end—the conversion of lost men to Jesus Christ and the greater glory and honor of God (cf. Matt. 5:16).

The primary task of the church is to bring people to Christ and teach them to be his disciples. Yet the church also has subsidiary but still vitally important tasks including social service. At the same time such duties should always be seen as serving a higher end—the apostolate. In Acts 6:1–7 deacons were set aside to minister to the physical needs of people, but at least two of these deacons, Philip and Stephen, became missionaries after their diaconal work was completed.

Dietrich Bonhoeffer is very helpful in the distinction that he draws between the penultimate and ultimate. The church, he contends, must relate itself to both dimensions—the crucial issues that concern man's livelihood in the world and also the final questions that pertain to man's eternal destiny before God. According to Bonhoeffer, the penultimate exists only for the sake of the ultimate, otherwise it would remain purely worldly activity. He also insists that the penultimate should be seen in light of the ultimate, lest any means be justified in the accomplishing of worldly goals. The two dangers are going directly to the ultimate and losing sight of the ultimate. The Law of God may be associated with the penultimate and the gospel with the ultimate. We must be concerned both with God's Law as it bears upon the burning issues of life in this world and the gospel, which deals with man's eternal salvation. To preach either the Law or gospel alone is to give men a truncated gospel.

Unfortunately, many churches are concerned neither with the ultimate nor the penultimate but with the trivial. A church supper is given more weight than racial peace in the community or the salvation of men's souls. It was against immersion in the trivial that Paul declared: "For the kingdom of God does not mean food and drink but righteousness and peace and joy in the Holy Spirit" (Rom. 14:17). On the other hand, even trivial concerns do not remain so when they are directed toward spiritual ends, namely, the reconciliation of men to God and to their fellowmen. This is why Paul could also advise: "Whatever your task, work heartily, as serving the Lord and not men, knowing that from the Lord you will receive the inheritance as your reward; you are serving the Lord Christ" (Col. 3:23, 24; cf. 1 Cor. 10:31).

Though we should naturally be attentive to the things of this life, our chief concern must be for the kingdom of God and his righteousness (Matt. 6:33). We need to give serious heed to this admonition of a contemporary social prophet, William Stringfellow: "Human justice is not a substitute for divine justification."[9] Because he saw that the Word of God was not central in the activities of the East Harlem Protestant Parish in New York he was compelled to sever his ties with that organization.

Yet the theological priority of justification and regeneration should not be confused with chronological priority. Sometimes we must minister to the physical and material needs of men before we bring them the message of salvation. William Booth had for his motto "Soup, soap, and salvation." He saw that hungry and dirty derelicts will not be interested in our message until we demonstrate Christian kindness and deal with their immediate needs.

Jesus healed the sick and fed the hungry, but he had a spiritual purpose—to bring men to the realization of their spiritual sickness and their spiritual hunger and of the living God who can meet these needs. He was angry that the people who had been fed with the loaves and fishes did not see the sign in the miraculous meal (John 6). He admonished his hearers to labor not for the food that perishes but for the food that endures to eternal life.

Jesus was a frequent visitor at the home of Mary and Martha, the two sisters of Bethany (Luke 10). On one occasion when Martha chastised her sister Mary for not helping her with the preparation for the meal our Lord reminded her that the one thing needful is hearing and contemplating the Word of God. Yet Marys need to become Marthas just as Marthas must first be Marys. The Christian who hears the Word and reflects upon it must share the fruits of his contemplation in outgoing service to the needy. He must bear witness to the love of God in Jesus Christ both through the demonstration of a Christian life and the proclamation of the gospel. He will be a Good Samaritan but only because he was first of all a worshiper of God in the temple.

NOTES

1. Jacques Ellul, *The Presence of the Kingdom,* trans. Olive Wyon (Philadelphia: Westminster Press, 1951), p. 47.

2. Helmut Thielicke, *Theological Ethics* Vol. I, ed. William H. Lazareth (Philadelphia: Fortress Press, 1966), p. 507.

3. Dietrich Bonhoeffer, *No Rusty Swords,* trans. Edwin H.

Robertson and John Bowden (New York: Harper & Row, 1965), p. 225.

4. Paul Ramsey, *Who Speaks for the Church?* (Nashville: Abingdon, 1967).

5. Reinhold Niebuhr, *Christian Realism and Political Problems* (New York: Charles Scribner's Sons, 1953), p. 110.

6. Note that the reference here is to polity, not doctrine or theology.

7. William H. Lazareth, "The Weber Memorial Lectures" in *The Bulletin of Moravian Theological Seminary* (Fall, 1968), p. 9.

8. See H. Richard Niebuhr, *Christ and Culture* (New York: Harper & Bros., 1951).

9. Quoted in Daniel Williams, *The Spirit and Forms of Love* (New York: Harper & Row, 1968), p. 254.

4

The Missing Dimension

Oh, let us never forget this, let us not reduce the spiritual to the worldly. Even though we may earnestly think of the spiritual and the worldly together, let us forever distinguish them.

SØREN KIERKEGAARD

THE SECULARIZING OF THEOLOGY

If there is anything that characterizes modern theology, it is the loss of a spiritual or supernatural perspective. These two terms are correlative, since spiritual means to be centered in God, and the God of the Bible transcends both earth and the heavens. His glory is exalted above the heavens and towers over the earth (cf. Ps. 57:11; 108:5; 113:4, 6; 1 Kings 8:27). Yet the dominant emphasis in the new theology is on an immanental God, one who is pictured as the life-force of the universe or the world-soul or the depth of existence.

Harry Blamires in his *The Christian Mind* maintains that the modern western world is witnessing the eclipse of the Christian mind, one that "looks beyond this life to another one." He goes on to describe the features of such an outlook: "It is supernaturally orientated, and brings to bear upon earthly considerations the fact of Heaven and the fact of Hell."[1]

In the Bible God is Spirit (John 4:24), and he is to be sharply distinguished from the world of temporality and relativity. He is a personal Being who stands above the world, who created the world, and who is basically not dependent upon the world. He is not a creative process nor an ideal of pure reason nor simply the "power of the future."

Moreover, the kingdom of God is a spiritual kingdom, one that does not fit into this world. Jesus said to Nicodemus: "Truly, truly, I say to you, unless one is born of water and the Spirit, he cannot enter the kingdom of God. That which is born of the flesh is flesh, and that which is born of the Spirit is spirit" (John 3:5, 6). And he goes on to declare: "If I have told you earthly things and you do not believe, how can you believe if I tell you heavenly things?" (v. 12).

Though man's outward form is fashioned out of the material, he is basically created by the Spirit of the living God. It is perhaps more true to say that man partakes in the Spirit than that he has a spirit. At the same time I believe that man is a spirit as well as a body and that his real self, the self-transcending ego, is to be distinguished from his bodily form. That such language is palpably unacceptable in many theological circles today is only another sign of the vast extent of the secularization of theology.

Instead of seeing man's hope as the heavenly Jerusalem (Heb. 12:22; Rev. 21:2), modern secular theology sees it in terms of the secular city (Gibson Winter, Cox) or a progressive egalitarian society (Alves, Garaudy, Moltmann). Instead of viewing the new world order as being ushered in by the personal return of Christ from heaven, avant-garde theology sees it as being inaugurated by wars of liberation and revolution. It can be said that heaven has been secularized into a utopian goal on earth.

It is becoming fashionable to hold that the kingdom of God is distinguished from the present world by its futurity rather than by its ontological transcendence. George Linbeck exemplifies the modern view: "For the Bible, the great divide is not the vertical ontological contrast between material and immaterial, natural and supernatural but the horizontal, temporal contrast between the two ages of the same world's history."[2] Yet this serves to obscure the infinite qualitative gulf between the Creator and the creature, between God and the world, the heavenly and the earthly. It tends to deny that the world has a beginning and an end, that there will be a new earth and a new heaven.

Nowhere is the gulf between biblical orthodoxy and the new theology more evident than in the doctrine of God. Moltmann has declared that the understanding of God as "the authority in heaven" is past and prefers to speak of God as "the power of a qualitatively new future."[3] Gregory Baum, avant-garde Catholic, argues that divine transcendence can no longer refer "to God's independent existence in a supernatural world," but it must now be reinterpreted to signify "the deepest dimension of human history and the cosmos."[4] For Herbert Braun, the radical Bultmannian, "God" is merely a form of human interrelatedness, a convenient expression for the hidden, vital impulse within man to live creatively and responsibly. Edward Scribner Ames has described God as "an order of nature" which includes man and "all the processes of an aspiring social life."[5] No longer having divine revelation for its object, theology is reduced in many circles to the study of man, history, or nature.

What characterizes the current theological scene is the re-emergence of monism, the philosophy that holds that all of reality is of one piece, that there is no world beyond this one. In former times monism took the form of idealism, but in the recent past it has appeared in a naturalistic guise, though idealism continues as a live option.

Schleiermacher, one of the fathers of the new theology, held that "it is folly to make a distinction between this world and the next. Religious persons at least know only one."[6] For him the divine is essentially the ground of all finite being and comes to self-consciousness in human nature. The only immortality that we should be concerned with is what "we can now have in this temporal life."[7]

Tillich, who leans heavily upon Schleiermacher as well as Hegel, conceives of God as the ground of being and describes his position as an "ecstatic naturalism." Since he thinks of God as Being-itself rather than process, he is probably closer to the tradition of idealism. It can be said that he seeks to transcend traditional naturalism by idealism or mysticism. The same can be said for Bultmann, who has declared: "The contrast between here and beyond, and thus the contrast between naturalism and supernaturalism, must be overcome. God must be recognized as the Unconditional in the conditional."[8] What is important to recognize is that both of these theologians deny the existence of a personal transcendent being who is independent of the world and of a heavenly realm that lies beyond this world.

In Pannenberg also we see the rebirth of a kind of idealism, after the pattern of Hegel. Pannenberg's philosophy has been described as a form of panpsychism in which God's presence permeates all of history. History "is constituted by the presence of the infinite in the midst of the finite." He holds to the undivided unity of history and nature in the thought of God. There is only one world: nature and history permeated by the divine presence. Against the neo-orthodox view that God revealed himself absolutely and irrevocably in the one particular event of his becoming man in Jesus Christ, Pannenberg believes that God reveals himself only indirectly in the totality of all the events of history. It is well to note that this theologian rejects the concepts of the supernatural, sacred history, the supra-historical, and miracle. He repudiates miracle because it is in tension with the concept of creation. What we find in Pannenberg, as in Tillich and Bultmann, is a one-story universe, and God is its depth or ground.

In a manner not dissimilar to Pannenberg, Gordon Kaufman has constructed a system that can only be described as a kind of historical monism.[9] His God transcends the present world but not history. All of reality is of one piece—historical. His God is both temporal and historical, not supernatural. He is caught up in the striving of his creation for fulfillment.

Another hallmark of the new theology is pan-sacramentalism. This means that God's presence is discerned in and conveyed through everything. This often borders on pantheism in which God is identified with the world or panentheism in which God is inseparable though distinct from the world. Altizer terms his position a "dynamic-process pantheism." His God becomes progressively actualized and real in history. For Tillich the divine spirit is the ultimate dimension of depth in the human spirit.

A pan-sacramentalistic or pantheistic orientation also implies a loss of distinctions between the holy and profane, the spiritual and secular. For William Blake, who had a great influence on Altizer, "everything that lives is Holy." Schleiermacher avowed: "All that is human is holy, for all is divine."[10] The Catholic philosopher Michel Quoist has said that "nothing is secular in the world." For J. A. T. Robinson the incarnation means that "all things" can be called "holy."[11] Neo-Hegelian R. J. Campbell declared that "the whole cosmic process is one long incarnation and uprising of the being of God from itself to itself."[12] This new emphasis is also glaringly apparent in a remark of Ronald Gregor Smith: "The eternal is in time, heaven is through earth, the supernatural not other than the natural, the spiritual not more than the wholly human."[13]

Even the early Barth was not immune to the pantheistic spirit of the modern age. In his *Epistle to the Romans* (2nd ed.) he declared that "everything natural is holy by that very fact, because the Holy, too, is natural." Von Balthasar, a sympathetic Catholic critic of Barth, calls this a "theopanism." At the same time the dialectic theology as it developed sharply challenged both the Hellenistic and modern distortions of Christianity, though it was not in the end able to reverse the drift of modern religion toward pantheism and relativism.

Outside of the school of dialectic theology some other theologians too have spoken out against the secularization of religion in our time. Mention should be made of P. T. Forsyth who constantly warned against an amalgamation of the faith with philosophy, but Forsyth like Barth is now in partial eclipse, though his writings are currently being promoted in conservative evangelical circles.

Still another hallmark of the new theology is the loss of the concept of miracle. Schleiermacher averred: "Miracle is only the religious name for event. Every event, even the most natural and common, is a miracle if it lends itself to a controlling religious interpretation. To me all is miracle."[14] When everything becomes a miracle, of course, then the original meaning of this concept has been dissolved.

Modern theology is characterized too by the loss of the idea of an absolute or definitive revelation from God in history. For Schleiermacher, "Every original and new communication of the Universe to man is a revelation . . . every such moment of conscious insight."[15] Ernst Troeltsch maintains in his *The Absoluteness of Christianity* that we can hold to the Christian faith as normative but not as absolute. He rules out any claim to a final revelation of the absolute in a particular time and place in history. His position becomes more relativistic and also syncretistic in a later essay where he writes: "The Divine Life within history constantly manifests itself in always-new and always-peculiar individualisations."[16]

On the current scene we can point to the Roman Catholic theologian Louis Evely, who maintains that faith cannot be based on miraculous happenings in history but only on the present experience of the Spirit of God—an experience which is universal and available for everyone. In his view the man of today "believes only that which he himself sees, verifies, and experiences. He is not taken in by appeals to authority, or by the opinions of 'experts.' "[17] He asserts that though we cannot have certain knowledge of a divine revelation given once for all times, we can have a broken perception of spiritual reality in the encounters of life.

Even Frederick Herzog, who makes a conscious attempt to remain loyal to biblical norms, including the historical particularity of the gospel, cannot escape the immanentalist and anthropocentric mood of the times. In his *Liberation Theology* he declares: "Jesus liberates man from the question of the after-life and future resurrection, to concern for unoppressed life. . . . Resurrection takes place now as freedom from oppression. . . ."[18] And again: "Manhood is not to cast itself upon the absolute outside itself, but to acknowledge in itself every dimension of transcendence and future that religion otherwise objectifies as being outside of men."[19]

For modern theology, man, even the man of faith, is not called to render a definitive witness; rather he is embarked on a quest or venture. Every claim that he can make concerning the truth is relative and fallible. This means that the church can no longer speak with authority, since it has ceased to have an absolute norm or standard.

The sad state of modern theology is reflected in these words from the inaugural address of Robin Scroggs, professor of New Testament at the Chicago Theological Seminary:

We are thus in no secure place. We have found no single authoritative standard from the past of what to say or how to live. Neither have we a secure self-understanding erected on the basis of our immediate experience. We in fact find ourselves in the abyss of a continual uncertainty, but we are kept from falling into chaos by the very tension between past and present . . . We have no assurance that where we happen to be is the best or final place to stand.[20]

Naturalism, relativism, and mysticism are very much in vogue in modern theology and philosophy. For C. Lloyd Morgan, God is the emergent process viewed as "directive Activity." In the thought of Henri Bergson, God is the vital urge expressing itself in the creative activity of the evolutionary sequence. Troeltsch, after the manner of Hegel, speaks of "the self-transformation of God into nature and creature" and of these "being re-transformed into spirit by means of redemption."[21] Teilhard de Chardin has declared: "Christ saves. But must we not hasten to add that Christ, too, is saved by evolution?"[22] For Albert Schweitzer all of reality is grounded in a unitary life-force which he calls "the Creative Will whence all life emanates."

For modern naturalism, including that which claims to be religious, the empirical world of becoming is the only reality. For the idealists the world of becoming is only an appearance, a mask of eternal Being. But both groups are united in affirming that there is only one reality, whether this be process or idea.

The one other alternative open to the moderns is to posit an underlying unity which ties together idea and process, subject and object, but we are then in the camp of mysticism. Many of the theologians and philosophers that have been mentioned gravitate eventually toward mysticism. Even secular theologians like J. A. T. Robinson now uphold what they call a "secular mysticism."

In mysticism there is no conceptual content to truth. As Schleiermacher expressed it: "The true nature of religion is neither this idea nor any other, but immediate consciousness of the Deity as He is found in ourselves and in the world."[23] The hallmark of mysticism is immediacy over the Word. In the mystical experience reason is negated and transcended. The ground of being is viewed as the undifferentiated unity, beyond good and evil. The mystics continue to affirm the Absolute, but they are very likely to reject the Christian claim that the Absolute has appeared in a final and definitive way in history. The mystical Absolute is an impersonal ground of being or soul of nature. Christianity in contrast affirms the concrete absolute, Jesus Christ. In mysticism the eternal God calls to the eternal within man. In the Christian faith the eternal becomes man.

The concept of a finite God has also entered into modern theology and philosophy. Here can be mentioned William James, Edgar Brightman, Edward Scribner Ames, Alfred North Whitehead, Schubert Ogden, Bernard Meland, Henry Nelson Wieman, Daniel Williams, Charles Hartshorne, Teilhard de Chardin, and Nikos Kazantzakis among many others. Whitehead, the dean of process philosophy, has declared: "It is as true to say that God creates the World, as that the World creates God."[24] Instead of the majestic Creator-God of Holy Scripture Whitehead upholds a creative life-force struggling to fulfillment within the world process.

Kazantzakis reflects the current mood in these words: "Our God is not almighty, he is not all-holy, he is not certain that he will conquer, he is not certain that he will be conquered."[25] In flagrant opposition to his Greek Orthodox heritage he avers: "God needs us, not out of love, but because we are the flesh through which he lives and grows."[26] His God is the creative force within man that needs to be released by the will to self-affirmation and power. The utterly pagan orientation of his thinking is evident when he exclaims that "it is not God who will save us—it is we who will save God, by battling, by creating, and by transmuting matter into spirit. . . . Life is a crusade in the service of God. Whether we wished to or not, we set out as crusaders to free—not the Holy Sepulcher but the God buried in matter and in our souls."[27] Like Nietzsche, Kazantzakis champions a kind of Dionysian mysticism.

Theology and philosophy tend to reflect the spirit of the age (Zeitgeist), though an authentic biblical theology will invariably go counter to the mood of the times. The fact that the new theology is so much in tune with the present age is a poignant sign that it is not truly biblical but essentially cultural. The secularization of theology mirrors the secularizing of the culture. When God is reduced to an impersonal ground of being or to a life-force or creative process within nature, then the very meaning of the term God becomes suspect. The theologies of the impersonal Absolute and the finite God have prepared the way for the death of God and for the idea that man is God (as we see in Kazantzakis).

The death of God has also prepared the way for the birth of the gods, the mythological deities of the ancient world which are now reappearing in a new guise. We are witnessing today the rise of the cults and the recrudescence of gross superstition. We can mention in this connection the current fascination with astrology, Satanism, witchcraft, flying saucers, reincarnation, spiritualism, and hallucinogenic drugs. With the demise of the supernatural in theology and philosophy, men are beginning to yearn and seek for the supernatural, though they can reach by their own power only the preternatural, the borderland between earth and heaven. The only transcendence available to man is a transcendence within immanence. Even in the cult of spiritualism the other world that we supposedly make contact with is acknowledged as being simply another dimension within the space-time continuum.

The most that man can attain by his own power is a poignant awareness of the mystery of life or of the ground of meaning in life. God is still experienced, not as the Savior from sin, but as the Abyss, the Void, the Nothingness. It should be noted that in the circles of secular existentialism one speaks of the "encounter with Nothingness." The true God can be known only as he gives himself to be known. We have not discovered the supernatural until we have been confronted with the Creator-God of biblical faith who revealed himself fully and decisively in Jesus Christ. The vision of the absolute in popular mysticism, occultism and much modern-day existentialism is a product of man's idolatrous imagination; yet this can only be recognized as such in the light of biblical revelation.

TWO MISUNDERSTANDINGS

The current plight of theology can only be understood against the background of the two conflicting world views that have consistently infiltrated Christian theology. The first of these, which we shall call the classical, posits an antithesis between the spiritual and the physical. This is not supernaturalism but dualism. Plato posited the worlds of being, nonbeing, and becoming; the last is simply a combination of the first two. It was said that the present world is a mixture of form and matter and the goal in life is therefore to extricate oneself from the material and ascend to the spiritual. The body is pictured as the prison house of the soul and therefore constitutes an obstacle to the soul's salvation. The spiritual man will seek to free himself from the bonds of the flesh in order to be reunited with the world soul or the eternal.

The classical idea is basically dualistic, but it can take the form of monism in which the phenomenal world is seen as a visible manifestation or appearance of the spiritual or ideal world. The trend toward monism is more apparent in Aristotle's philosophy and in Neo-Platonism than in Plato.

In this kind of orientation God becomes the demiurge or the impersonal soul of the universe. In Aristotle the concept of God and the idea of the Good are combined, but this God is static and impassible, the Unmoved Mover. In Plotinus deity is the transpersonal and ineffable One beyond temporality and relativity. For the Stoics God becomes the Divine Reason of the universe.

The classical view of life and the world entered into the thinking of the church fathers resulting in a marked compromise with biblical insights. In place of the living personal God of biblical faith medieval theology tended to uphold a God whose love is directed toward himself rather than toward the creature and who is basically unaffected by the suffering in the world. He is more or less the self-contained Absolute, the goal of man's earthly pilgrimage but One who does not share our trials and afflictions. To be sure, many devout Christians lived in the patristic and medieval periods

—men and women who had a deep personal faith in a living God—but any surge toward biblical piety was often subverted by philosophical and theological speculation. The classical view of God and the world left its imprint upon the life of devotion, for it turned man's attention away from the temporal and earthly to the spiritual and supernatural. In man's pursuit of the heavenly world, this world was depreciated and denigrated. A dualistic asceticism became dominant in which the soul was depicted as being imprisoned in a corruptible body and exiled in a vale of tears and death.

It can be said that in the development of Catholic thought service in this world was subordinated to contemplation of the ideal or heavenly world. This is acknowledged by Father Hans Urs von Balthasar: "The patristic period viewed contemplation as a participation in heaven, as an end in itself, and considered ordinary Christian living as little more than a preparatory phase, a means of attaining the necessary purity of heart, while the Middle Ages regarded it as a kind of inferior receptacle into which the exuberant riches of contemplation discharged themselves."[28]

This is not to discount the presence of evangelical voices in the early church and medieval periods in which biblical motifs sometimes were more evident than Platonic ones. Surely the depreciation of the material world and the call to detachment are much more obvious in Dionysius the pseudo-Areopagite, Origen, Jerome, and John Scotus Erigena than in Bernard of Clairvaux or in Thomas Aquinas, who regarded the apostolic life as superior to the purely contemplative life. Yet even Thomas could ask in all seriousness "whether our atmosphere is the demons' place of punishment."

Again we should note that leading theologians like Augustine and Aquinas often succeeded in modifying and even transforming Greek philosophical concepts in the light of the gospel. In upholding God as Creator and Lord of the universe, these theologians and others added the dimension of transcendence to the concept of eternity. The Forms of Plato, the Intellect of Plotinus and the self-thinking thought of Aristotle are supratemporal, but none of them is utterly transcendent because none is wholly outside of and infinitely superior to a world created *ex nihilo*.

While the classical view regarded the spiritual as opposed to the physical, the modern view sees the spiritual as another side of the physical. The modern heresy can take the form either of naturalism or idealism, but these prove to be two sides of the same coin. The spiritual is simply the material under another name, or the material is only an appearance or manifestation of the spiritual. The modern view is illustrated in these words of Santayana: "There is only one world, the natural world, and only one truth about it; but this world has a spiritual life in it, which looks not to another world but to the beauty and perfection that this world suggests, approaches and misses."[29]

In the modern view spiritual worship becomes service to one's fellowman. For St. Paul, service to our neighbor is a means to the adoration of God who is Pure Spirit. We are called to serve our fellowmen precisely so that God may be glorified (Rom. 15:1–6). If there is no transcendent or spiritual dimension in our service, then it is none other than humanitarianism.

The idea of God undergoes a drastic transformation in the modern view. God is now seen as a "Will-to-Love" imbedded in the universe (Albert Schweitzer) or a process within nature (Henry N. Wieman) or a presence within history (Leslie Dewart). For Teilhard de Chardin God is the "soul of the world"; for J. A. T. Robinson he is the "depth of being." Joseph Mathews of the Ecumenical Institute simply describes him (or it) as the "ongoingness of things." Kazantzakis sees God as the primordial force within the world and man which drives man to surpass himself. The God of the modern view does not transcend the universe but is in the words of William James the "higher part of the universe" or the spirit of the universe. Wieman sees God, which he has called "creative interaction" or "creativity," as transcendent only in the sense that its possibilities are unlimited. On another occasion he has described God as "the Process of Progressive Integration."

Other theologians and philosophers who conceive of God

as basically immanental are Thomas Altizer, John Cobb, Schubert Ogden, Henri Bergson, Charles Hartshorne, Bernard Meland, Fritz Buri, Gregory Baum, J. A. T. Robinson, Fred Brown and Harvey Cox. Pannenberg and Tillich seek to posit a transcendence within immanence, but their God is simply the depth of being or the power of the future, not the Holy One who stands over and beyond the world and man.

Whereas in the classical and scholastic traditions there was an appeal to rational clarity and the power of logic, the moderns more often appeal to observation and human experience. The empiricist approach of the later Enlightenment has proven more potent in the contemporary world of thought than the classical rationalistic view which was still very much evident in the Renaissance. D. C. Macintosh reflects the modern view when he contends that revelation is nothing other than "the discovery of reality through experience."[30] So does Wieman in this remark: "God is an object to be perceived through sense experience."[31] The moderns are prone to base their case on facts, on empirical evidence, not on innate ideas or external authority. This can be seen not only in the logical empiricists and neo-naturalists but also in some of the neo-fundamentalists. While maintaining a firm grasp on the essentials of the faith, conservative scholar John Warwick Montgomery seeks to buttress biblical claims by an appeal to the norms of historical science. Even Pannenberg, despite his rationalistic bent, maintains that truth is discovered through "historical analysis" not by abstract reflection.

The appeal to mystical experience is also very much present in modern theology and philosophy, though some would want it to be tested by empirical norms. In this respect one can discern an affinity between men of such divergent views as Schleiermacher, Tillich, Altizer, and Meland. Others more in the world of philosophy proper who might be mentioned in this connection are Teilhard de Chardin, Alan Watts, Alfred North Whitehead, Martin Heidegger, D. H. Lawrence, and Karl Jaspers. In contrast to the neo-Platonists these men generally uphold not a world-despising but a world-affirming mysticism.

The essentially immanental God of neo-Protestant and

neo-Catholic theology stands in contrast to the God of classical philosophy who is wholly other, who is not related to the world. It also contradicts the impassible God of medieval theology, the self-contained Absolute who remains unmoved by man's earthly afflictions.

In the classical view the material or the secular is annulled. In the modern view it is enthroned or divinized, or at least it is seen as partaking in the divine. Not all the modern thinkers that have been mentioned, of course, completely exemplify the modern heresy, since we are thinking in terms of "ideal types." At the same time the modern view is reflected to a high degree in the many persons to whom we have referred. It should also be recognized that both these misunderstandings will probably always be with us in one form or other.

THE BIBLICAL VIEW

The biblical view stands in contrast to both Hellenic idealism and modern naturalism. It avoids both an ahistorical mysticism and a this-worldly reductionism. It gives significance to history, but it also affirms a reality beyond the horizon of history.

The biblical perspective is neither monistic nor dualistic but theistic. But this is not a rational theism in which we arrive at our conception of deity by abstract reflection but a biblical theism in which the idea of God is adduced from a special, historical revelation. As against both monism and dualism, the Bible affirms only one ultimate reality, the triune God, but also a secondary, contingent reality, his creation. Matter is a channel of the power of God but not an aspect of his nature.

In the biblical understanding God is essentially transcendent, but he condescends to our level in the person of Jesus Christ. He infinitely transcends the world, but he is not distant, as in Hellenistic philosophy and deism, for he identifies himself with our sufferings and makes his abode among us (John 1:14). Yet this is the immanence of personal encounter, not a pantheistic immanence. God is immanent not as a world soul or a creative energy but as the divine companion (cf. Ps. 16:8; 23:2, 4). Our emphasis should not be that God is "in here" or "out there" but "right here," as our covenant partner. The Spirit of God upholds and undergirds the world more than suffuses it. He does not exist so much in the depths of our being as by our side in our daily struggles.

The biblical God is essentially independent of the world, not wholly dependent nor interdependent. But he enters the world in his freedom and relates himself to us in love. The Word is not an eternal idea or transcendental ideal but a living Person who enters into our history and takes on flesh (John 1:14).

The biblical God is neither the "Directive in history" (Wieman) nor the "divine dynamic of history" (Günther Gassmann) but the divine Lord who is sovereign over history. Yet he realizes and demonstrates his sovereignty within history. What the Bible upholds is neither the abstract, timeless God of Greek speculation nor the finite, temporal God of modern religious naturalism but the personal-infinite God who condescends to our level while still remaining sovereign over the world.

A biblical, evangelical theology will affirm the immutability of God but not in the sense of classical philosophy. God's immutability means that he does not change in his innermost intentions. His truth is immutable not as a timeless idea that exists in its own right but as a divine plan or purpose that cannot be annulled. Immutability does not rule God but serves him. The true God does not change because he wills not to change and does not deem it good to do so— not because he lacks the power to change.

The Bible also portrays God as "the Almighty," but the biblical view of omnipotence must be distinguished from the philosophical idea of *potestas absoluta* (absolute power) which became prominent in medieval scholastic theology. The omnipotence of God does not mean that he exercises arbitrary, unrestricted power but that he rules over his creation in the spirit of justice and love. He is not the sole cause of all that happens but the divine Lord over all that happens. The idea of *potestas absoluta* cancels out all creaturely independence and leads finally to pantheism or theopanism.

Again the Scriptures affirm the omnipresence of God. But this idea must not be taken to mean that God's being literally permeates all matter but that everything is included in his overall vision (cf. Prov. 15:3). God is with us but not a part of us. He is present to all his creatures but not intermingled with the creaturely. Barth rightly says that omnipresence does not mean spacelessness but God's freedom to be in space.

In the Hebraic-Christian view the spiritual does not oppose the material but transcends it and enters into it. One might say that the spiritual stands in juxtaposition to the material. While the spiritual signifies the world that is unshakable and eternal (Heb. 12:27, 28), the physical belongs to the passing aeon, to the old world order that is destined to pass away. The prophet declares: "All flesh is grass. . . . The grass withers, the flower fades; but the word of our God will stand forever" (Isa. 39:6, 8).

The physical body is not denigrated, but its role is restricted to this world. The author of 2 Peter affirms: "I think it right, as long as I am in this body, to arouse you by way of reminder, since I know that the putting off of my body will be soon, as our Lord Jesus Christ showed me" (2 Pet. 1:13, 14). Paul declares: "It is sown a physical body, it is raised a spiritual body. If there is a physical body, there is also a spiritual body" (1 Cor. 15:44).

In the biblical view the spiritual not only transcends the earthly but also transfigures it. In Romans 8:10, 11 the spirit and body are distinguished, but the body is said to be given life through the Spirit. The material is taken up into the spiritual and elevated by it. In contradistinction to the classical view Scripture affirms the resurrection of the body and a new heaven and a new earth. The material is not rejected or discarded but transformed. Though the outer shell of the physical body will remain, at death the inner core is taken up into a new body which will be the heavenly vessel of the spirit. Paul uses the illustration of the seed of wheat to point to the basic continuity between our physical and spiritual bodies (1 Cor. 15:36 f.). Some of the early church fathers gave the illustration of the caterpillar and butterfly to illumine the mystery of this continuity.

While the Greeks posited the inherent immortality of the soul and the moderns tend to deny human immortality, biblical faith speaks of the immortality of a personal relationship with God. Its view of immortality does not rest on the Platonic notion of the indestructibility of the soul but rather on the saving work of Jesus Christ who by his resurrection from the grave conquered the power of death. Because of God's grace and promise to deliver by virtue of the work of Christ, man can be assured of victory over death.

In the biblical view the old earth will be destroyed by fire because of the sin of man (2 Pet. 3:7, 10–13), but this destruction will also signify its transmutation into a new earth. This will be more than a restoration: it will be a new creation. The biblical view opposes both the Orphic and Platonic myth of eternal return and the modern myth of perpetual progress. Instead it sees a catastrophic end to earthly history and a new world coming down from heaven (Rev. 21:1, 2).

For biblical Christianity the opposite of the spiritual is not the bodily or physical but rather the flesh or the "old man." The flesh signifies not the body as such but man in his frailty and weakness, creaturely existence corrupted by sin. The flesh connotes the selfish, the sensual, and the carnal. Moreover, the flesh can take spiritual forms such as enmity, vanity, greed, and the lust for power. The antithesis of the spiritual is the sinful, not the earthly. And the sinful more often than not signifies the perversion of the spiritual.

The earthly, on the other hand, is the vessel of the spiritual. It is neither the enemy of the spiritual nor a substitute for the spiritual. What opposes the spiritual is the earthbound.

The secular should not be arrayed against the spiritual, for this again connotes the Hellenistic misunderstanding. Instead the secular should be seen as the field of action for the spiritual. It is the preoccupation with the secular or the enthronement of the secular that contradicts the spiritual. The secular has spiritual significance but not divine status. We are not called to celebrate and venerate the secular per se but instead the spiritual incarnation in the secular as seen in Jesus Christ.

In the New Testament our physical body is not a prison house of the soul but a "temple of the Holy Spirit" (1 Cor. 6:19). Paul declared: "For no [normal] man ever hates his own flesh, but nourishes and cherishes it" (Eph. 5:29). (The reference here is to the physical body.) Paul admonished his hearers to discipline their bodies, but he opposed the dualistic asceticism which regarded the body with disdain and which renounced sex as the embodiment of sin. Francis of Assisi reflected the biblical viewpoint when he described his body as "Brother Ass," something that needs to be cared for and often bridled but never mistreated.

In the Scriptures grace transcends nature; however, the antithesis is not between grace and nature but between grace and sin. Grace does not so much complete nature as renew and alter it. That is to say, it turns nature in a new direction.

The criterion for truth in the Christian view is neither the world nor thought but the Word. And it is faith, not reason, that perceives the Word. As Luther avowed: "The Word must be believed against all sight and feeling of the understanding."[32] Such a remark stands in sharp contradiction to both the Renaissance and Enlightenment, but it is patently true to the Scriptures.

We need today to recover the distinction between the holy and the profane, the spiritual and the secular, the revelational and the rational. Bonhoeffer protested against their separation, but he never confused them. He declared: "And yet what is Christian is not identical with what is of the world. The natural is not identical with the supernatural or the revelational with the rational."[33] Modern secular theology unfortunately has lost sight of these crucial distinctions in its enthusiasm for the secular.

The spiritual does not oppose the secular, but it is necessary that the two be distinguished. The spiritual side of man is the whole man in relationship to the living God. The secular side of man is the whole man in relationship to the world. When the secular is grounded in and informed by the spiritual, then man is free to live as a Christian in the very midst of the world.

A spiritual problem is whenever the soul or body of man

is threatened with dire injury. The body too has spiritual significance, since it is the vessel of the soul. All problems that touch upon the survival and well-being of man in the world are spiritual, but they are not always recognized as such. The Christian will see them in a different light from secularized man, namely, in relationship to God and his commandments. While the sociologist will interpret the mass adulation of dictators in terms of social pathology, the Christian will recognize it as idolatry. Whereas the secular psychologist may diagnose an illness as acute depression, the believer will see it as oppression by the devil. These views do not necessarily conflict, and ideally they should complement one another. Yet one's understanding of any problem or issue is markedly deficient unless it is seen in the perspective of eternity (*sub specie aeternitatis*). The secular perspective may be valid on its own level, but when it pretends to be ultimate or absolute then it is arrayed in opposition to the spiritual.

The secular has a certain autonomy in the eyes of biblical faith, but its autonomy is relative and therefore limited. It derives its legitimacy and significance from the spiritual. Moreover, its ground and goal are in the spiritual, in the living God himself.

THE CHURCH'S SPIRITUAL MANDATE

"Spiritual" means to be centered in the God who is both holy and infinite. It therefore has a dual signification—directed toward holiness and toward eternity. Bonhoeffer helped us to recapture the first connotation but not the second. There is need today for a new statement on the meaning of eternity and the supernatural.

Karl Barth pointed us in the right direction when he defined eternity not as timelessness but as the fulfillment of time. Barth, true to his biblical heritage, spoke of a divine timefulness as over against a timeless idea or pure thought.

While there is not an absolute dualism between eternity and time, the supernatural and the natural, there remains a distinction. The natural is taken up into the supernatural; time is taken up into eternity. Eternity signifies the transcendence of time and nature as we know it, but not necessarily their negation.

Moltmann and Pannenberg have also made an attempt to reinterpret the "eternal." Moltmann speaks of eternity in terms of "the extremity of time" and the fullness of time. This can be helpful except that he refuses to posit a higher space and time beyond the sphere of earthly history. He and some others could benefit here from the labors of Karl Heim who has sought to utilize the insights of modern science in arguing for the reality of what he calls a "suprapolar space" or a "space of eternity."[34] Heim's position is surely in accord with the biblical testimony which speaks of eternity as a "high and holy place" (Isa. 57:15).

Pannenberg too has tried to reinterpret the concept of eternity.[35] For him "all events coincide in an eternal present." Eternity is "the truth of time," "the unity of all time." Eternity is "the concurrence of all events in a single present." He speaks of "the eternal depth of time" but refuses to affirm the reality of a heavenly world that stands in juxtaposition to this world. It seems that despite his emphasis on history he is moving in the direction of an ahistorical mysticism. Eternity does not break into time but is ever-present within time. In his view eternity is more a quality of time than another kind of space-time.

It is right to criticize a false otherworldliness that disregards life in this world, but we must affirm a true otherworldliness that gives significance to life in this world. The classical view was otherworldly in the false sense, and the modern view is exclusively this-worldly. The biblical view sees this world in light of the world to come and as a preparation for it.

Our mandate as Christians is to prepare men for life with God in eternity. But this preparation takes place here and now. It can therefore be said that the church has a sacred mission in a secular world.

Our gospel is not derived from this world but is given from heaven (John 6:33; Gal. 1:11, 12). It concerns a kingdom that is not of this world (John 18:36; Phil. 3:20). The new birth is not of this world but is instead a miracle of grace. It means being born from above (John 3). It refers to a spiritual, not a physical birth. The otherworldly orientation of the Christian faith is underscored in John 17:14: "I have given them thy word; and the world has hated them because they are not of the world, even as I am not of the world."

Yet the Christian is not called out of the world. Our Lord declared: "I do not pray that thou shouldst take them out of the world, but that thou shouldst keep them from the evil one" (John 17:15). And again: "As thou didst send me into the world, so I have sent them into the world" (17:18).

We have a spiritual mandate in the world, one that is to be lived out in the agonies, trials, and sufferings of our fellowmen. The Christian ideal is the spiritual in the secular, not the spiritual in the abstract but in the concrete. As Bonhoeffer put it: "The antithesis between the world and the Church must be borne out in the world."[36] And in the words of Cardinal Jules Saliège: "The Kingdom of God is not of this world, but it is in this world that it is won."

Christianity does not teach detachment from the sufferings and evils in the world. On the contrary by confronting the holy God we are awakened to the evils both within ourselves and in the world and are impelled to correct them. G. C. Berkouwer declares: "The vertical dimension of the Gospel does not relativize the horizontal concerns of faith; rather, the vertical dimension forces us to awaken to the urgent and inescapable demands of the horizontal dimensions of life."[37]

Christianity is not only a way *to* life but also a way *of* life. It begets a subculture of its own, a style of life which runs counter to the mores and values of any given society. The Christian should not withdraw from the world but battle with the principalities and powers of the world.

Like her Master the church must seek to be incarnate in the world, but it will always be an alien force, a "colony of heaven" in the world (cf. Phil. 3:20). Just as the world persecuted and crucified her Lord, so the church too will suffer persecution by the world. Even its self-giving service will be misunderstood and will bring upon it the reproach of sin-ridden men.

Emmanuel Mounier, the French personalist, anticipated much of the new emphasis when he maintained that the mission of the church, "which is not of this world, must be accomplished in this world."[38] At the same time Mounier was adamant that this mandate is still a spiritual one. It is to bring men to Christ and to spread his gospel to the whole creation. "Even as the Church refuses the separation of the two worlds [spiritual and temporal], so she affirms their vigorous distinction."[39]

Corporal works of mercy have a place in the church's mission, but they are to prepare men for a spiritual message. The church is first of all a mission venture, not a social welfare agency nor a political lobby. Yet its missionary message has tremendous cultural and political implications. John Mackay, known for his social involvement, has declared that "the purpose of the Church is not to create a new order" but rather to "create the creators of a new order." By preaching the message of justification and regeneration the church can be instrumental in creating a new kind of man who will then begin to set society right.

This brings us to the priority of prayer and evangelism. As the apostle said, the end or purpose of our faith is the salvation of souls (1 Pet. 1:9). Our ultimate goal is the greater glory of God. Yet the saving of men's souls is precisely what gives glory to God. So also does the adoration of God in prayer. Jesus seemed to regard the adoration of God as taking priority even over the service of the poor and ailing (cf. Luke 5:15, 16; John 12:1–8).

Yet our spiritual commission certainly includes social service. Good Samaritan service, even social action, should be seen as a fruit and evidence of a living faith in God. Occasionally it may also be viewed as a stepping stone to such faith.

The gospel concerns itself with the whole of man's life but not equally. Inward regeneration is deemed more important than outward or material security (cf. Acts 6). Clarence Jordan, who started a movement to provide low income housing for the very poor, nevertheless saw that man's deepest need is not for shelter nor even food. He avowed: "Man is not just a belly in search of bread. He's a soul in search of God."[40] For Jordan, the physical and material things of life should be seen as tools of the kingdom, a trust from God.

Social relevance is established by the preaching of the commandment of God while evangelical power is found in the preaching of the gospel of reconciliation. Sometimes the church must address itself to the concerns of this life before it points men to the ultimate solution, Jesus Christ. But it should always strive to see this-worldly concerns in the light of the ultimate concern. Our social protest as well as our works of charity should be imbued with a spiritual motivation and purpose. As Calvin said, the love of neighbor "seeks its cause in God, is rooted in him and is directed toward him" (*comm.* John 13:34).

The theologies of revolution and liberation go astray when they uncritically accept the Marxist dictum that the wrongs of the world can be corrected by altering man's social environment. The decisive seat of evil is not in the social and political institutions but in the weakness and imperfection of the human soul itself. What man most desperately needs is a new spiritual horizon and a new inward motivation, and this is where the church has its greatest opportunity.

It is not inequity but unbelief that is the gravest sin afflicting men today; indeed, the latter is the root of the former. Man is plagued with hardness of heart, and this is a spiritual malady. The only remedy is a spiritual medicine, the gospel of Jesus Christ.

Evangelism has priority but by itself is not sufficient. It must be supplemented and fulfilled in Christian service. Jesus attacked the Pharisees who "preach, but do not practice" (Matt. 23:3; cf. Matt. 7:21). The apostle declared: "But if any one has the world's goods and sees his brother in need, yet closes his heart against him, how does God's love abide in him?" (1 John 3:17). He goes on to say: "Little children, let us not love in word or speech but in deed and in truth" (v. 18). Yet he was speaking about a spiritual, not a natural love. And such love is the fruit of a living faith in a holy God (1 John 5:1, 2).

NOTES

1. Harry Blamires, *The Christian Mind* (London: S.P.C.K., 1966), p. 67.

2. George Linbeck, *The Future of Roman Catholic Theology* (Philadelphia: Fortress Press, 1970), p. 13.

3. Jürgen Moltmann, *Hope and Planning* (New York: Harper and Row, 1968), p. 51.

4. Quoted in James Hitchcock, *The Decline and Fall of Radical Catholicism* (New York: Herder and Herder, 1971), p. 53.

5. Edward Scribner Ames, *Religion* (New York: Holt, 1929), pp. 176–177.

6. Friedrich Schleiermacher, *On Religion* (New York: Harper and Row, 1965), p. 20.

7. Ibid., p. 101.

8. Rudolf Bultmann, et al., *Translating Theology into the Modern Age*, ed. Robert W. Funk (New York: Harper & Row, 1965), p. 91.

9. Gordon D. Kaufman, *Systematic Theology: A Historicist Perspective* (New York: Charles Scribner's Sons, 1968).

10. Schleiermacher, *On Religion*, p. 180.

11. J. A. T. Robinson, *Liturgy Coming to Life* (Philadelphia: Westminster Press, 1960), p. 33.

12. Walter M. Horton, *Contemporary English Theology* (New York: Harper and Bros., 1936), p. 34.

13. Ronald Gregor Smith, *The Whole Man* (Philadelphia: Westminster Press, 1969), p. 111.

14. Schleirmacher, *On Religion*, p. 88.

15. Ibid., p. 89.

16. Ernst Troeltsch, *Christian Thought: Its History and Application* (London: University of London Press, 1923), p. 14.

17. Louis Evely, *The Gospels Without Myth*, trans. J. F. Bernard (Garden City, N.Y.: Doubleday and Co., 1971), p. 61.

18. Frederick Herzog, *Liberation Theology* (New York: Seabury Press, 1972), p. 156. Despite our very different thrusts I stand with Herzog in his concern for biblical foundations in theology and in his plea that the church identify itself with the afflicted and oppressed.

19. Ibid., p. 153.

20. Robin Scroggs, "Tradition, Freedom, and the Abyss" in *The Chicago Theological Seminary Register*, Vol. LX, No. 4 (May, 1970), pp. 12, 13.

21. From his *Glaubenslehre*, quoted in H. R. Mackintosh, *Types of Modern Theology* (London: Nisbet and Co. Ltd., 1949), p. 191.

22. Quoted in *Triumph*, Vol. VI, No. 9 (Nov., 1971), p. 2.

23. Schleiermacher, *On Religion*, p. 101.

24. Alfred North Whitehead, *Process and Reality* (New York: Simon and Schuster, 1960), p. 116.

25. Nikos Kazantzakis, *The Saviors of God* (New York: Simon and Schuster, 1960), p. 116.

26. Kazantzakis, *The Odyssey: A Modern Sequel* (New York: Simon and Schuster, 1958), p. 793.

27. Kazantzakis, *The Saviors of God*, p. 106.

28. Hans Urs von Balthasar, *Prayer*, trans. A. V. Littledale (New York: Sheed and Ward, 1961), p. 228.

29. Quoted in W. Warren Wagar, ed., *Science, Faith, and Man* (New York: Harper and Row, 1968), p. 98.

30. D. C. Macintosh, *The Reasonableness of Christianity* (New York: Charles Scribner's, 1925), p. 126.

31. Henry Nelson Wieman, *The Wrestle of Religion with Truth* (New York: Macmillan, 1927), p. 94.

32. Martin Luther, *Sermon on John 3:1–15,* quoted in Karl Barth, *Church Dogmatics* I, 1 (Edinburgh: T. & T. Clark, 1949), p. 253.

33. Dietrich Bonhoeffer, *Ethics,* ed. Eberhard Bethge (New York: Macmillan, 1965), p. 199.

34. See Karl Heim, *Christian Faith and Natural Science* (New York: Harper and Bros., 1953).

35. W. Pannenberg, *What Is Man?* (Philadelphia: Fortress Press, 1962), pp. 68–81.

36. Dietrich Bonhoeffer, *The Cost of Discipleship* (London: SCM Press Ltd., 1959), p. 239.

37. In *Christianity Today,* Vol. XII, No. 25 (Sept. 27, 1968), p. 70.

38. See Emmanuel Mounier, "Christian Faith and Civilization" in his *The Spoil of the Violent*, trans. Katherine Watson (West Nyack, N. Y.: Cross Currents, 1944), Section II, p. 16.

39. Ibid.

40. Clarence Jordan, *The Substance of Faith*, ed. Dallas Lee (New York: Association Press, 1972), p. 58.

5

How Christians

Can Change the World

If we don't keep indoctrinating, we lose the vision. And if we lose the vision, we become merely philanthropists dealing out palliatives.

DOROTHY DAY

THE CHRISTIAN VOCATION

The division in the church today revolves at least partly about the role of the Christian in the world. Should the Christian be a conscious effector of social change or should he be a witness to the gospel in his ordinary tasks in life? Should he be directly involved in the revolutionary struggle for liberation from social oppression, or should he be primarily concerned with personal salvation? That there is no unanimity on these questions is simply an indication that the church today is torn by a profound theological disunity. It is also a sign that theology has not done its homework in respect to the biblical understanding of the Christian vocation.

In the New Testament Christians are called to be the light of the world and the salt of the earth (Matt. 5:13, 14). It is not only the Word that we bring that is the light, as the Reformers contended, but we ourselves are to be light and salt. We are to fulfill this divine imperative in our words and in our lives. We are to bring enlightenment and to lighten the burdens of others. Too often Christians are prone to join the world in attacking the political and religious establishments. Yet it is not enough to curse the darkness; we must also light a candle if the world is really to be changed.

It is not laid upon the Christian to be the honey of the world (as George Bernanos reminds us) but the salt, and salt stings when applied to the wound of the infection of sin. Our mandate is not to sweeten and sugar the bitterness of life but to expose this bitterness to the light of the cross, for there can be no true healing without pain. Salt is of no use if it remains in the saltcellar, and light is of no use if it remains hidden under a bushel. The salt must be united with the dough of the world so that it can preserve the world from decay and death. The light must be carried into the darkness so that the threatening power of hidden evil may be taken away. Salt and light have this in common: they expend themselves and are sacrificed when mixed with something else, i.e., dough and darkness. To be light and salt is therefore the opposite of a religiosity which lives only unto itself.

A closely related metaphor that describes the Christian vocation is leaven in the lump (cf. 1 Cor. 5:6, 7; Matt. 13:33). We should be peacemakers and reconcilers and thereby revitalize and stabilize the wider community in which we live. The church should be the white corpuscles that take out the infection in society.

Again our Lord commissions us to be fishers of men (Matt. 4:19). As fishers of men we are to let down the net of the gospel, and the gospel itself will bring in the fish. This is to say we are to be heralds of the faith (Matt. 28:19, 20) and thereby instruments of the Holy Spirit in the saving of souls.

The image that Jesus uses more often than any other to describe the meaning of discipleship is that of the lowly servant. When our Lord washed the feet of his disciples, he was giving to them an example of self-giving service (John 13:14–16). A disciple is not greater than his Master (John 15:20), and if we are to follow in his steps, we must be willing to be servants who minister unto others (cf. Gal.

5:13). In our society today the emphasis is on being a winner. Self-fulfillment is the goal, not self-denial, but the Christian must stand against the stream of the culture in upholding the ideal of the self-sacrificing servant.

It is also well to recognize that the elect of God are sent into the world as sheep amid wolves (Matt. 10:16; cf. Ps. 44:22; Acts 20:29; Heb. 13:13). The sheep is a defenseless animal, and this means that it offers nonresistance to its evil adversary. But the paradox is that in self-sacrifice and in refusal to strike back, the little flock of the faithful are instrumental in bringing about the defeat of the forces of evil. By refusing to fight fire with fire, by giving our enemy food and drink, we are actually heaping "burning coals upon his head" (Rom. 12:20), which means filling him with guilt and shame. To fight the wolves with their own weapons is to join the wolves. To be eaten by the wolves is to give them indigestion and thereby create within them an internal change so that they will become more like sheep. In my opinion the New Testament does not advocate an absolute pacifism, since very often the sheep must wear a mask for the sake of the preservation of society. But in regard to their own rights and privileges Christians are called to give up what they have when challenged by the powers of darkness and attacked by evil men. The principle of no retaliation is not a law for the secular order, but it is the law of the kingdom of God.

Finally, we should never forget that the elect of God will be marked as strangers and exiles in this world (Heb. 11:13; 1 Pet. 2:11). Just as the world hated Christ, so it will hate his disciples (cf. Matt. 10:22; John 15:18–20). Even when the people of God attain positions of power and responsibility in society they will be distrusted as aliens, as indeed they are, for their ultimate allegiance is not to the state or the political party but to God. Even when God's people partake in the blessings and comforts of the world, they will not feel at home in this world, for they will forever be sensitive to the abiding evils in society and in men which threaten to undermine every personal and social gain.

The Christian vocation entails witnessing by a style of life as well as by the proclamation of the truth. This twofold dimension in Christian discipleship is reflected in these words from a letter of Francis of Assisi to the General Chapter of his Order: "He has sent you all over the world so that you should bear witness to his voice in word and deed, and have everyone learn that there is no one almighty but he."

The commission of the Christian is not to withdraw from the world but to try to change the world. It is not the Stoic "courage to be" but the courage to overcome that characterizes the Christian life. J. Gresham Machen has put this very well: "Instead of obliterating the distinction between the Kingdom and the world, or on the other hand withdrawing from the world into a sort of modernized intellectual monasticism, let us go forth joyfully, enthusiastically, to make the world subject to God."[1]

THE GOSPEL PROCLAMATION

The Christian is enjoined to speak the truth with love and boldness (*parrhesia*). And it is the truth of God that transforms man and makes him into a new creature. When men hear the glorious gospel of reconciliation and redemption, then they are changed inwardly and are moved to give of themselves to their neighbor in a spirit of love. It is through the preaching and hearing of the gospel that the Holy Spirit chooses to accomplish the miracle of conversion (cf. Rom. 10:8–10; 14–17; 1 Cor. 1:21).

When we contend that the Christian must bear witness to the gospel, we mean the whole gospel, and this includes the Law. But Law by itself, including the civil law, cannot change man. The most that the law does is to restrain his rapacity. Laws are necessary for survival and order in this world, but it is the kerygma, the good news, that gives to man a new vision and motivation.

What is needed is not simply an improved social environment but a new kind of man. I make this asseveration against some of the current theologies of liberation which contend that oppression is basically rooted in social systems rather than in men.[2] Evangelical Christians cannot accept the position of Marx: "Man is simply matter in motion without spirit, soul or free will. As such he is not responsible for his actions. His beliefs, endeavors, religion and culture are a mere reflection of his economic environment, and all the evil that man does is a product of that environment." In the view of biblical faith man is responsible, and it is the abuse of his God-given freedom that produces an oppressive environment. It is interesting to note that the neo-Marxist Herbert Marcuse seems to be moving away from a rigid economic determinism. He contends that the truly free society "can never be a mere by-product of new institutions and relationships, no matter how basic." It can be achieved only through "a new type of man, a different type of human being, with new needs, capable of finding a qualitatively different way of life, and of constructing a qualitatively different environment." The young Karl Marx also saw that the problem lies in man himself. He declared: "To be radical is to grasp things by the root. But for man the root is man himself."

The contemporary Russian novelist Solzhenitsyn maintains against Marxism that the individual man takes priority over the collective man. While Marxism seeks to lend dignity to man by changing his exterior economic conditions for the better, Solzhenitsyn gives voice to his Christian convictions by affirming that man can achieve dignity only by penitence which engenders purity in the inner self.

For modern secular humanism, including Marxism, the poison of racism can be removed through social reform and education. Biblical Christianity sees this problem in a different light. The real enemy is racial and cultural pride, not ignorance. And behind this pride is unbelief, hardness of heart, what the Bible calls original sin. The solution is spiritual regeneration, not egalitarian education. This entails repentance for the collective sin of white racism. Laws are necessary to protect the defenseless, but they can only hold the dyke against sin. It is the gospel alone that takes away sin, and this means that the final solution to racism as to other social ills is biblical evangelism.

Not all Christians, of course, have the gift of gospel preaching. There is a diversity of gifts and services, and preaching is one of the most important, but by no means the only gift. Yet all Christians are called to be witnesses, and this entails speaking openly about Christ as well as serving in self-giving love.

SERVICE IN DISCIPLESHIP

Not only are we called to be missionaries, ambassadors, heralds, fishers of men, but also servants, leaven, salt, and light. The mandate placed upon us is to take up the cross and enter into lowly discipleship. We should not only proclaim the message of the cross but also bear the cross, and this means to bear the burdens of others (Gal. 6:2).

Discipleship under the cross consists essentially in Good Samaritan service. It entails ministering to the outcasts, feeding the hungry, clothing the naked, and visiting those in prison (cf. Matt. 5:43 f.; 25:31 f.; Rom. 12:20; James 2:14–17; Titus 3:14). Jesus himself not only preached the kingdom message but also healed the sick and fed the hungry. And we are called to walk in his steps (1 Pet. 2:21), to follow after him.

Deeds of loving-kindness in association with the Word can also be a means of grace, a means of conversion. Unbelieving husbands can be won over to the gospel by the reverent and chaste behavior of their wives (1 Pet. 3:1, 2). Paul wrote to the Corinthians that they themselves are letters of recommendation (2 Cor. 3:2, 3). By the example of their lives the message of Christ is "known and read by all men." "Good deeds are conspicuous" and "cannot remain hidden" (1 Tim. 5:25). Or as the Heidelberg Catechism affirms, we "by our reverent behavior may win our neighbors to Christ" (Q. 86).

It should be recognized that Good Samaritan service is not done for its own sake but for the sake of the advancement of the kingdom of God. Service is done in love, but it is done for the sake of mission. Our motivation is compassion, but our goal is evangelism. The Christian must seek the greatest good of his neighbor, which is his eternal salvation.

Martin Luther, who emphasized good works as the fruit of faith, maintained that their "final cause" is the moving of men to glorify God. As he aptly put it: "Because the heathen cannot see our faith, they ought to see our works, then hear our doctrine, and then be converted."[3]

Teresa of Avila, noted for her intense involvement in the social and political life of her day, saw all her works in the context of the gospel ministry. She declared: "The soul of the care of the poor is the care of the poor soul." She also said that when we show compassion to a sick person we should do it not for his sake alone but because "it is the will of the Lord."

As has been indicated, social service should be seen as both a stepping stone to the gospel and a fruit of the gospel. It is well to note that the manna and quails were given to the children of Israel in the wilderness in order to cause them to trust in God. This work of divine charity was intended to bring them to the Promised Land (Exod. 16). Our works of love must have this same goal. In our social service we prepare the soil so that the seed of the gospel can take root and grow.

Jesus saw his acts of mercy (feeding the hungry, healing the sick) as signs of the kingdom, and he was dismayed that the people were so slow to recognize them as such. His mission was to bring men into the kingdom of heaven, but they were content too often with material blessings. They welcomed Jesus as a political messiah, but they spurned him as the divine Savior from sin.

The integral relation between faith and works can be clearly seen when we realize that unloving actions and prejudice can be false stumbling blocks that keep men from the gospel. Acts done in a spirit of love will draw people to the gospel provided that they are truly exposed to the gospel message itself.

Social service by itself is humanitarianism. It is praiseworthy in the eyes of the world, but it does not cure the spiritual malaise that casts a shadow over all of man's works. Moreover, it even becomes dangerous when it is confused with kingdom service. It was against such confusion that the apostle warned that the kingdom consists not in food and drink but in righteousness, peace, and joy in the Spirit (Rom. 14:17).

Abraham Kuyper in his *Christianity and the Class Struggle*

contended that social service that is not rooted in the gospel may do more harm than good. To provide welfare benefits without a moral foundation can ultimately be disastrous. Indeed, a healthy person without a moral and spiritual purpose can be more dangerous than a sick person. Today we see a technology uncontrolled by moral principles threatening to destroy whole civilizations.

Many scholars contend on the basis of Matthew 25:31–46 that humanitarian concern is the indispensable condition for salvation. Yet a careful reading of this parable of the Last Judgment shows that people are accepted or rejected according to their attitude to Christ himself, and not simply on the basis of their social concern. The service that is performed to "one of the least of these my brethren" in verse 40 is service that is rendered to the messengers of Christ. Jesus does not have in mind service to the neighbor as such but service to those who bear his name (cf. Mark 9:41; Matt. 10:42). The response is not only to the messenger but to His message, for the two cannot be separated. Such a response would be manifest in the care that was shown to the physical needs of the apostles, who were often beaten, imprisoned, and starved in the course of their mission. The evidence of the response is loving concern, but the basis of the response is in the attitude of faith toward the messengers and the Word that the messengers proclaim. Certainly, the parable speaks of the obligation of the Christian to clothe the naked, feed the hungry, and visit those who are sick and in prison. And in relating this text to its wider context we can conclude that such acts of kindness should be done to all men and not just to the brethren in the Lord, though the needs of our brethren are especially to be considered (cf. Mark 9:41; Rom. 12:13; Gal. 6:10). Yet the Christian should do these good works in the name of Christ, and such action should be seen as the evidence and consequence of a living faith in Christ.[4] By no means should this parable be used as an argument for justification by works, since its intent is quite the opposite; nor is this notion present in any of the other parables.

Just as *diakonia* (service) serves mission so both *diakonia* and evangelism serve worship. The adoration and glory of

God is the overall goal of discipleship under the cross. Contemplation will drive us to action, but action in turn will direct us ever again to contemplation. In the view of P. T. Forsyth, "it is truer to say that we live the Christian life in order to pray than that we pray in order to live the Christian life."[5]

SOCIAL ACTION

The divine imperative entails not only deeds of personal kindness but also social service, and not just in the form of charitable and humanitarian works but in political action. Cullmann has rightly reminded us that the "principalities and powers" in Ephesians refer both to political forces and angelic powers behind them. We cannot always rely on the powers of persuasion, on the appeal to conscience and reason. We must sometimes bring political pressure to bear upon the situation.

Yet social action is not an integral part of the teachings of Jesus nor of Paul, though it is certainly implied in the gospel. Bultmann has said that "the Gospel knows nothing of 'social action' with its goals in this world. . . ."[6] But the gospel does create a climate for social action. Bultmann's existentialism tends to ignore this social dimension of the faith.

At the same time the New Testament gives a much more spiritual meaning to the concepts of deliverance, salvation and liberation than does the Old Testament. In Luke 4:18, 19 we find these oft-quoted words of Jesus dear to those who espouse a theology of revolution: "The Spirit of the Lord is upon me, because he has anointed me to preach good news to the poor. He has sent me to proclaim release to the captives and recovering of sight to the blind, to set at liberty those who are oppressed, to proclaim the acceptable year of the Lord." In the Old Testament source Isaiah 61:1, 2 the context is clearly political and social. But Jesus is definitely not thinking of political liberation as is indicated in Luke 7:22: "And he answered them, 'Go and tell John what you have seen and heard: the blind receive their sight, the lame walk, lepers are cleansed and the deaf hear, the dead are raised up, the poor have good news preached to them.'"

Jesus was not laying the basis for a theology of political liberation or revolution. His kingdom is not of this world, and this is why his message was a stumbling block to the Jews who yearned for a political messiah who would lead a rebellion against Roman rule. James Kallas makes a good case in his *The Significance of the Synoptic Miracles* that Jesus identified himself with the Danielic hope of a supernatural, eschatological kingdom over the Davidic hope of a Jewish this-worldly kingdom.[7] The liberation that Jesus was speaking about was salvation from sin. The captives are those who are enslaved to sin.

Alan Richardson warns against a misunderstanding of the mission of our Lord:

> It was not so much the possession of riches as one's attitude towards them and the use one makes of them which was the special object of Jesus' teaching and this is true of the biblical teachings as a whole. Jesus does not condemn private property, nor is he a social reformer in any primary sense; he is concerned with men's motives and hearts.[8]

James Cone, who sees Jesus as a political revolutionary and who upholds violence as a part of the Christian ethic, is doing an injustice to the real intention of our Lord. A redeeming feature of his black theology is that he seeks to make a place for God's wrath as well as his love. He rightly sees that the world is where people are dehumanized and that we are sent into the world to battle with principalities and powers, and this sometimes means the power structures of oppression. Yet when he urges men and women to be agents of God's wrath, then we must demur. One further criticism of Cone is that he makes the experience of a particular people (namely, the blacks) rather than divine revelation the criterion for truth and authority.[9]

At the same time the truth in the political theology of today should not be overlooked. This is that the gospel does have far-reaching social and political implications. The New Testament makes clear that the poor in spirit and also the economically poor are more ready to hear the gospel than the rich. Moreover, the gospel promises deliverance for the whole man, and this means from all that afflicts him— physical illness and deprivation as well as the spiritual disease of sin. In the total biblical perspective the promised liberation is not only from personal sin but also from sin in its social and cosmic dimensions, though there is no guarantee of this within history. The church has a spiritual mission, but the spiritual illumines and permeates all areas of existence.

Men of God will always take the side of the oppressed. They should show compassion to the outcasts and the despised. That God has a special concern for the poor and needy is illustrated in Psalm 72:12–14:

> For he delivers the needy when he calls,
> the poor and him who has no helper.
> He has pity on the weak and the needy,
> and saves the lives of the needy.
> From oppression and violence he redeems their life;
> and precious is their blood in his sight.

Through spiritual conversion Christians are set free to work for freedom from oppression and poverty in the social-economic sense. Our labors on behalf of the poor will not bring in the kingdom as the new Social Gospel contends, but they can be seen as a sign and witness of the coming kingdom. They should be regarded as a potent testimony to the Lordship of Christ. Yet full release from poverty and oppression will not be fulfilled within earthly history, for as Jesus said, the poor will always be with us (Matt. 26:11).

Where liberation theologies go wrong is by asserting that Jesus was dealing directly with political and economic problems in his message. They misinterpret him when they portray him as a social activist or political revolutionary. Jesus was a spiritual revolutionary. He rejected the Satanic temptation to be a worldly ruler (Luke 4:5–8). He was dealing with ultimate issues, with the problem of sin and the hope of eternal life.

Yet as we have said his message also has profound implications in the penultimate sphere. While Christ died for all men, he lived especially for some—the poor, the despised, the dispossessed. Yet in the New Testament the poor are never hailed as liberators or as the key to the world's hope. His message gives no comfort or support to utopians. He asked: "When the Son of man comes, will he find faith on earth?" (Luke 18:8). To be sure he promised that the meek shall inherit the earth, but he here has in mind the new earth beyond earthly history.

It is well to recognize that the early Christians were persecuted for standing by their faith, particularly for preaching the gospel. They were not engaged in a deliberate policy of civil disobedience. They did defy civil authorities when they refused to worship pagan gods, or when they resisted induction in the armed forces, which entailed the shedding of blood and homage to the Roman emperor. But they were by no means engaged in a conspiracy to overthrow the social order of that time.

The Christian should work in the social sphere—not for revolution or utopia but for laws that safeguard the rights of men. Laws are negative but necessary, for they restrain man's rapacity and also prepare the way for the gospel proclamation. Pascal said that those who do not fortify justice will end up by justifying force. And in the words of Reinhold Niebuhr, "Love without power surrenders the world to power without love." The Old Testament saints utilized power in the service of God and man, but they did so in their divinely appointed office in society. We think here of Moses, Joshua, Samuel, David, and Hezekiah. Conservative Christians need to be reminded that one cannot cure economic ills by appealing for "voluntary restraints." The pornographic industry, for example, is not hurt too much by calling on men of "good will" to avoid filth. Similarly real estate concerns will not buckle under and open their houses to racial minorities unless there are laws with teeth in them. To appeal to their compassion shows a lack of realism concerning human nature.

Niebuhr has said that we can change human behavior but not human nature. He is right that by social legislation we can only alter behavior patterns. But what neo-orthodoxy has been slow to acknowledge is that human nature can be changed by the preaching of the Word and the Spirit; this is to say, it can be turned in a radically new spiritual direction. Men can be given new motivations, new goals, a new attitude toward their fellowmen through faith in Jesus Christ. Spiritual regeneration is the key to lasting change in human behavior. Yet because regeneration is forever imperfect, laws are necessary even for the Christian.

At the same time we must bear in mind that social sanction has more weight than legal sanction. Public opinion is more effectual than laws that simply codify it. The inner change in attitudes and perspective is more significant than the outer change in laws. The Prohibition experiment failed in this country because not enough people were cognizant of the perils of social drinking and alcoholism and were thereby motivated to see that the law was enforced and obeyed.

Reinhold Niebuhr has also averred that order must be ranked before justice because without order there is no possibility of freedom. I agree with him here, for without order justice is an elusive dream. The Christian must support both "law and order" and "law with justice," though the former is only a means to the latter. Yet social justice as the world understands it must never be confused with kingdom righteousness, and Niebuhr would concur.

The church has a prophetic ministry, but saying the same thing that the world says is not providing leadership. We are not sent into the world to parrot the world's slogans or to approve the world's projects. We are to mix with the world without becoming absorbed in it. We are not to follow the world's agenda in our social action but God's agenda. Church councils which try to offer simple solutions to human problems should pay heed to 1 John 4:5: "They speak about matters of the world and the world listens to them because they belong to the world" (TEV).

We must not insist that there is a "Christian answer" to most broadly human questions. The gospel gives the ultimate answer, but not penultimate answers. It gives the final solution to the human condition. Yet Christians as concerned citizens must work for proximate solutions and limited objectives. We cannot bring in the righteousness of the kingdom, the brotherhood of love, but we can succeed in achieving always a higher degee of social justice.

By all means the Christian should beware of the perils of ghettoism and privatism. In one of Agatha Christie's novels an Episcopalian canon says: "See no evil, hear no evil, speak no evil—and what is more, think no evil! That should be the motto of every Christian man and woman." The canon is perhaps unknowingly referring to the famed monkeys of Buddhist piety that close their eyes and ears to all discord and evil. This strategy also resembles that of Christian Science, Unity, and the School of Positive Thinking. It has great appeal in the circles of the economically and culturally privileged, for it tends to shield the conscience from the burning wrongs in society. The Christian is summoned to involvement in the world, not to detachment or isolation. One creates good not by avoiding evil but by recognizing it and bringing the power and might of the Spirit of God to counteract it. Instead of following the three monkeys, we should heed these words of the prophet: "Learn to do good; seek justice, correct oppression; defend the fatherless, plead for the widow" (Isa. 1:17).

Yet our social action must be Christian social action, and this means that it should not serve the human craving for power. It should have its roots in God's grace and its goal in God's kingdom. Otherwise it becomes ineffectual and even detrimental. Therese of Lisieux reminds us in her *The Story of a Soul:* "You discover that trying to do good to people without God's help is no easier than making the sun shine at midnight." Martin Luther King wisely saw that social action must have a spiritual basis and motivation if it is to have permanent fruits. He realized that desegregation "will break down the legal barriers and bring men together physically, but something must touch the hearts and souls of men so that they will come together spiritually."

Just as the Christian should spurn the way of ghettoism so he must avoid utopianism or perfectionism. The slogan of the New Left, "Make love, not war" is questionable particularly when it is seen as a substitute for hard and sometimes harsh political decisions that are backed up by the coercion of law. Niebuhr reminds us that the radical law of love cannot be directly applied to the social order. Luther's attitude should also be given serious attention: "I have often taught thus, that the world ought not and cannot be ruled according to the gospel and Christian love, but by strict laws and with sword and force, because the world is evil. It accepts neither gospel nor love, but lives and acts according to its own will unless compelled by force."[10] Perhaps Luther too easily separates the gospel of love from the laws that rule the world, but his realism should be appreciated in a time when criminals are viewed as victims of a bad upbringing and rioting students as well as rioting police are seen as lacking only in sound judgment. In our view Christians are sometimes called to use the ways of the world to accomplish limited social objectives but always under the criterion of love.

Luther often spoke of the strange work of love done by God. He believed that Christians too are called to exercise this strange work of love on occasion. This means that the Christian must sometimes resort to force not in order to promote the kingdom of God or in defense of his own rights but in defense of the helpless and the downtrodden. Christians must sometimes be sheep in wolves' clothing, remembering that the "sons of this world" are wiser than "the sons of light" (Luke 16:8). We should not hesitate to use "the wisdom of serpents" in dealing with serpents even though we should combine this with "the innocence of doves" (Matt. 10:16). Love must be united with cunning if we are to make an impact on the kind of world in which we live. Christians who are sheep in wolves' clothing will collaborate with the power structures, even though they will inwardly stand outside of them. They are still sheep because their goals and values are radically different from those of the world.

The strange work of love does not mean using the works of the devil to cast out the devil (cf. Mark 3:23). It does not entail rendering evil for evil (cf. Prov. 20:22; Rom. 12:17). But it does mean using the lawful ways of the world to restrain the rapacity of the world. These are ways that pertain to the fallen creation, not to the new creation. The use of force may well be necessary at times, but force for the Christian must be always a servant, never a master. The Christian should avoid deliberate evil, but he cannot avoid the taint of evil if he is to fulfill his social and political obligations in society.

The Christian may even find himself caught up in a violent revolution, but he must never commit himself wholeheartedly to such a revolution. Moreover, he should never uphold revolution as a Christian answer or much less as a way of salvation.[11] No revolution is ever justified in the sight of God, and this is especially true for one that is undertaken in the name of the gospel or the church. Yet a revolution by violence may become inevitable because the oppression may become humanly intolerable, though for Christians even the worst of human conditions can be endured with the aid of divine grace. Ellul says that if the Christian does use violence he "cannot either feel or say that he is justified; he can only confess that he is a sinner, submit to God's judgment, and hope for God's grace and forgiveness."[12]

How different is the current theology of revolution which upholds violence as a Christian way of life. Sergio Arce Martinez, president of the Matanzas seminary in Cuba, states that "revolutions in all times constitute . . . the road to making concrete the Kingdom of God in a determinate moment of history, and revolutionaries are nothing else but 'servants of the God on High.' "[13] While he admits that revolution is a destructive force and finally dehumanizing, it can be supported because "it will more radically destroy all that which confronts it as an opposing force." He consequently subscribes to the Marxist dictum that the end justifies the means, but this is not permissible for a Christian who seeks to follow the New Testament.

Nonviolent resistance is closer to the ideal of love and can even be united with this ideal. Yet even here there is a tension, since pure love cannot easily be reconciled with political pressure or human manipulation. Politics will always involve compromise. As responsible citizens and concerned Christians, we should seek to make a creative compromise, and though falling short of perfect love, this way is far better than detachment from the evils and sufferings of the world. Nonviolent action is also a compromise, since strikes and boycotts will always cause injury to some party or other. The Christian ideal is not nonviolent resistance but nonresistance (cf. Matt. 5:39) and returning good for evil (Rom. 12:17–21). We can follow this ideal in our personal dealings, where our own safety and welfare are concerned, but where the welfare of others is at stake we have a new moral situation. Here a compromising action will be necessitated, even where this entails the way of nonviolent resistance or pacifism. Even noncombatant medical service in the armed forces is a compromise, since in this way we are giving aid to soldiers who are sent forth to kill.

It is an open question whether the New Testament advocated an absolute pacifism. When the soldiers asked John the Baptist what they should do, he replied: " 'Rob no one by violence or by false accusation, and be content with your wages' " (Luke 3:14). Just as the forerunner of our Lord did not disarm these soldiers so Jesus did not disarm the centurion, but he did prohibit his disciples from using force in the defense of his kingdom (Matt. 26:52). He also pointed to the folly of violence when he declared that "all who take up the sword will perish by the sword." In Romans 13 Paul reminds us that the state derives its power to wield the sword from God and that Christians are subject to the governing authorities. Yet in the same chapter he points the Christian to the sixth commandment which prohibits killing. Jean Lasserre in his *War and the Gospel* contends that the Christian must obey the state up to this point, where it commands him to take the blood of his neighbor.[14]

My position is that both the pacifist and nonpacifist strategies entail a compromise with the ideal of absolute love, and one must simply decide on the basis of his own conscience which kind of compromise is the lesser. In our day where warfare involves weapons of mass destruction and indiscriminate killing, the pacifist option would definitely seem to have the sanction of God, though the conscientious objector must not claim that he thereby escapes the taint of sin through his actions. A pragmatic pacifism which takes into account the realities of the human situation would seem to be closer to the Christian ethic than a doctrinaire pacifism.

The unique weapons of the Christian even in his secular

vocation are prayer, the Word of God, and love. Only by these means can the gospel be spread and can the kingdom of God take concrete form (cf. 2 Cor. 10:4). Yet insofar as the Christian still lives in the old aeon and insofar as he is a sinner, the ballot box and political pressure can also be legitimate weapons. They do not serve to bring in the kingdom, but they do serve to restrain the forces of evil. Whether the sword can be a legitimate weapon when exercised by the police or the armed forces is a thorny theological question, as we have already intimated, but surely force can be used when it does not entail outright killing. It is interesting to note that the British police generally carry clubs but not guns, and they seem to be remarkably efficient. Yet in an extreme situation, when no other alternative seems possible, life sometimes has to be taken, but again we should not claim that this is fully in accord with the ideal of love or that such action is ever praiseworthy before God.

The Christian is called to the way of spiritual violence, to the violence of love. Ellul rightly maintains that by demolishing a regime's moral justifications, spiritual violence effects more significant change than any other. It is incumbent upon the Christian to fight the spirit underlying the violence of men, and this is where the real change must occur. The violence of love must not be confused with a worldly concept of powerlessness which may be just as corrupting as the misuse of power. Such love is characterized not by weakness but by the meekness which overcomes through singleness of heart and total dependence on God (cf. Matt. 5:5).

Yet even as spiritual revolutionaries we cannot save the world nor bring in the kingdom, though we can effect a measure of social change. We can prevent society from plunging into chaos and thereby contribute to its survival, but we cannot transform society into the new Jerusalem. We should also bear in mind that success is not our mandate but obedience. A Christian agent of social change is not necessarily one who initiates change by starting a new organization. He is one who brings the divine imperative to bear upon public affairs in his words and in his life.

In his political *diakonia* the Christian must resist the

temptation to embrace a particular party line. He must be able to discern what is morally right and wrong in every program and platform. The evangelical Christian should certainly side with Muskie over Agnew on their diverging analyses of American prisons, for here is a moral issue that transcends party affiliation. While Agnew has maintained that "our penal system remains among the most humane and advanced in the world," Muskie told a Governors' Conference in Puerto Rico (1972) that our prisons are "monstrous, inhuman dungeons, schools for crime and centers for sexual abuse." The Christian is free, however, to support any politician on the right on another occasion and on another question.

Both Calvinists and democratic Socialists oppose the rightist capitalist dictum that the government which governs least is the best. Yet a government that encourages its people to place their security in itself is also opposed by Calvinism. Reformed Christianity will stand against both statism and laissez-faire, and this means that an earnest Christian in this tradition will always be an alien force in the ranks of the right and the left. He will be a "stranger and exile" even in the party that he supports for the present.

Christians in their secular vocations should be encouraged to engage in social action. Their political involvement is part of their civil calling, though I would argue that it is not part of their distinctly Christian calling.[15] If the church as a church tries to impose its will on the state, then we have the phenomenon of clericalism. The church should give moral guidance to the state through its social ethic. This is not its first or primary business, but it may be part of its wider mission.

Should the church as a church provide low income housing for the poor, since this entails not only proclamation but implementation as well? My position is that this is more clearly the responsibility of the state and of Christians working in government. Yet in an emergency situation, when the poor are being left homeless, and when the state cannot or will not act, then the church may direct its funds towards this purpose, though only in the service of its primary mission. When benevolence money is diverted away from missions for such purposes, however, then the church may be guilty of a grave dereliction of its duty to fulfill the great commission.

Social activists often deride church people for expending all their energies on Good Samaritan service rather than on politics. Yet we should bear in mind that Good Samaritan service, understood as loving care for the downtrodden and despised in society, is invariably more difficult than political action, because it is more demeaning. The routine, boredom, and lack of recognition in such work put off those who are enamoured with what is fashionable and glamorous. It can be said, therefore, that such service entails a greater degree of personal sacrifice. Many who are willing to march in picket lines would not dream of changing the bedclothes of disease-ridden persons in mission hospitals or in ministering to alcoholics and drug addicts in rescue missions. Still less would they be willing to give their time and energies to the care of lepers, epileptics, the mentally retarded, the physically deformed, etc. Such self-giving service entails super-human love, the spiritual love that goes out to all men without any thought of return. While any responsible citizen is willing to enter the political arena, only the man who is born again from above is willing to soil his hands and possibly also his reputation in ministering to the poor and despised in society. Social action is important, and a Christian is derelict if he tries to avoid it, but the church should always point to the priority of Good Samaritan service and gospel evangelism.

Lights in a Dark World

The Christian community is a colony of heaven in a hostile world (Phil. 3:20). Its authentic members will go counter to the latest trends in the culture and stand out as lights in a sea of darkness. Their style of life will conflict with the life-style of technocratic culture. We are not to be conformed to the world but transformed by the renewing of our minds (Rom. 12:2).

The church today must point to the priority of being over

doing. This is especially important in an age in which activism is the norm. It is indeed a revolutionary stance, since for the world, what matters is to *act,* not to *live.* The two virtues of the technological society are efficiency and utility, but these are not necessarily Christian virtues. These are the ideals of a pragmatic business culture. Christians need to uphold the virtues of prayer, study, contemplation, and silence. This is not to take the pathway of the hippies, since Christianity defends withdrawal only for the sake of deeper penetration into the world. Prayer, moreover, is the highest work because it means wrestling with God and prevailing through God. This stands in marked contrast to the contemplation of oneself or of nature which is eulogized by what Charles Reich calls "Consciousness III."

Biblical Christianity does not denigrate work, but it sees work as a means to glorify God and not simply to expand technology. Moreover, the work that is purposeful and meaningful must be grounded in faith and prayer. Work does not justify us before God, but the proper kind of work can be an evidence of the state of justification in which we already stand. The goal of our work is not to build the secular city of man but to herald the coming kingdom of God.

Can Christians truly change the world? John Wesley declared: "Give me a hundred men who will hate sin and nothing else, and fear God and nothing else, and I will change the world." He did not mean that he could build the kingdom of God on earth, but he did believe that committed Christians could permeate the world with Christian values and influence and thereby make the world more receptive to Jesus Christ.

What we need to recover is a holy optimism which sees that the key to changing the world lies in the plan of God and the power of his grace. We should not give up the world to the powers of darkness in a spirit of defeatism, since we know that Christ is Lord over these powers. William Penn gave voice to this holy optimism: "True godliness does not turn men out of the world but enables them to live better in it, and excites their endeavors to mend it." To be sure, when society becomes unbearably corrupt, the only viable alternative for the professing Christian may be flight from the world, yet always with a view to returning at some future time with the light entrusted to him.

Our means should, of course, be consonant with our ends. Our weapons are the sword of the Lord, which is the Word of God, prayer, and devotion. But we must wield these weapons in a spirit of love, for otherwise they are to no avail. We need a baptism of the Spirit that will make us sensitive to the needs of the world and compassionate to the afflicted and dejected. As George Fox said, "O Lord, baptize our hearts into a sense of the conditions and needs of all men."

We need to identify ourselves with the suffering of the world, but not with its sin. We should be aware of the iniquity within man and the world, but we must always love the sinner. We must be realistic about human wickedness but compassionate in our attitude toward the wilful transgressor. As Martin Luther King has said, we need to combine a tough mind with a tender heart.

Christians must learn to swim against the stream and stand alone, sometimes even against the dictates of the church. Luther declared: "Redemption occurs in hope. It is in the process of becoming. Here we must stand, fence, and deal out blows. The coward is overtaken by disaster." This is the robust faith that is needed in our time.

It is also important to recognize that Christians must be dead to the world if they are to move the world. We cannot be open to the world's temptations if we are to be instrumental in liberating the world from its bondage. Only those who refuse to compromise with the world's values can turn the world to new values. It was not the theologians and clerics in the kings' courts that brought new life into the church and world in the past but the itinerant evangelists in their tents, the monks in their cloisters, and the pietists in their conventicles.

The churches should become beacon-lights, cities on the hill (Matt. 5:14, 15). They should not see themselves as a haven from the world but as a leaven within the world. The light that we have is not to be hid under the bushel but to be placed where all can see it.

Conservative evangelicalism has a firm grasp on the fundamentals of the faith, but in many other ways it has accommodated itself to the spirit of the world so that the real difference in being a Christian is obscured. Carl Henry has observed that "evangelical Christianity, for all its biblical vitalities, does not shape fellowships of redeemed persons to stand out in the world as community beachheads of the kingdom of God."[16] This is somewhat of an overstatement, since evangelical religious communities have arisen (e.g., L'Abri, Lee Abbey and Jesus Abbey) in which the world's patterns are sharply challenged.[17]

The church must speak in its councils to the problems of race and poverty, but even more it should try to solve these problems within its own community. Only when the churches themselves genuinely welcome people of other races and classes into their fellowships and also care for their poor and aged can they speak to the world with credibility and authority.

Racism should be recognized as a spiritual malady even more than a social pathology, and this is where the church can meet this problem. Racism is a form of unbelief, since it traces the values and gains in civilization to biological heritage and not to the grace of God. It is a disease of the heart which laws can hold in check but cannot erase. Blacks and other minorities are seeking equal rights, and these rights are much overdue. Some say that black people need to be more patient, but the church has not been impatient enough. The worship hour on Sunday mornings is still the most segregated hour of the week, and the churches should bow their heads in shame.

Liberal churchmen and some black power advocates see the end of racism in civil rights legislation, and such legislation is necessary, but they neglect the heart of the problem, which is sin against God. The solution entertained by many radicals (both on the left and right) in calling for the separate development of peoples to fulfill their special destinies denies the Christian principle that racial and class divisions are transcended through faith in the living Christ. By making race into an ultimate concern and by making the racial consciousness the criterion for truth, black power theologians and black separatists, as well as many white liberals, deny the human solidarity in sin, the historical particularity of divine revelation, and the universality of Christ's redemption. Racism can only be overcome when people become color-blind, when the black or brown person is seen first of all as an actual or potential brother in Christ and not as a member of a racial minority. But this can be accomplished only by an inward spiritual change.

Johannes Verkuyl of the Free University of Amsterdam, who has been active in the battle against racism, makes this astute observation in his critique of a certain kind of naïve liberalism:

> Why cannot "reason and science" ever make a real and funda-
> mental difference in such issues as the race question? It is
> because this kind of question is decided in the depths of human
> nature. The healing of relations between races is achieved only
> through rebirth, through radical conversion. The Holy Spirit
> Himself must bring about renewal and change.[18]

Christians also need to demonstrate a care for the poor, the neglected elderly, and the downtrodden in their own communities. To be sure, there are church homes for the aged, but these often prove to be a sign of the church's abdication of its responsibility to include these people in its wider mission. The cult of youth, which has infiltrated avant-garde theology, conduces to make the church insensitive to the needs of the elderly, especially the bedridden and those who are no longer "useful" in the eyes of the technological society. Are the poor, the ailing, and the aged being visited by their Christian brethren and are they included in our social functions? Are they being helped financially if their need requires such help? The early church practiced the sharing of goods so that no one was left needy or forsaken. The Mormons in this respect put evangelical Christians to shame, for they genuinely provide for their own.

There is a need today for lighthouses in which the light of God's truth can be seen in all its splendor and power. We are witnessing the rise of evangelical religious communities and retreat centers. Para-parochial fellowships are emerging like the Navigators and Young Life which carry the light into the

darkness of the world. But should not our colleges and seminaries also be lighthouses? If they do not or cannot fulfill
this role, should not new educational institutions be formed
with this purpose in mind? Indeed, should not the local congregation be a lighthouse, and if it is not, does this mean
that new kinds of congregations should be established?

Some Christians today see the hope of changing society in
Christian political parties that will seek to implement Christian principles in a secular context. Such parties have been
formed in several of the Scandinavian countries where a
militant and atheistic secularism threatens to erase Christian
values through governmental decrees. Such parties can le-
gitimately be supported by Christian laymen, but the most
that they can do is to hold the dyke against the sea of secularism. The penetration into the void of secularism has to
come some other way.

Emmanuel Mounier, the French personalist, who himself
was active in social concerns as a Christian layman, saw that
the church itself is most effective when it is being true to its
spiritual mission. He contended that "Christianity contrib-
utes more to the most material works of mankind when it
increases in spiritual intensity than when it loses itself in
problems of tactics and management." He recognized that
"Christianity is not directly oriented to the work of civilization," for its obligation is "to guide it . . . toward salvation."[19] Yet, men possessed with a spiritual vision will seek
to realize it in this present world. An inward spiritual revolution will result in a profound alteration of values and practices in society.

The spiritual vacuum today presents untold opportunities
for the church, but is the church fully prepared to fill this
vacuum? It can become prepared by emphasizing the
uniqueness of its message without neglecting its obligations
in the ethical area.

The two sins that the Old Testament prophets inveighed
against were apostasy and disobedience. They were also
adamant that apostasy or infidelity is the source of all injustice and inequity. Behind ethical failure and inequity are
unbelief and idolatry, and it is this spiritual relapse that the
church must confront today as never before. The rise of a

New Baalism and a militant humanism in our time signify the enthronement of man, and the church must unmask these movements for what they are—titanic rebellion against God. Too often in its enthusiasm for reconciliation the church tends to forget that we should be reconcilers of persons but not of ideas. The gospel cannot be correlated with the cultural ideologies of our time, for this would be apostasy on the part of the church.

T. S. Eliot has rightly said that the church can win over modern man only if it is "intellectually austere," "evocative of discipline," and "disdainful of transient fashions." Modern man, especially youth, is seeking for a faith that is challenging, not compromising. In its passion for relevance the church too often fails to tell it like it is and present a gospel that calls for a life and death decision.

Nowhere is the breakdown in morality today more evident than in the rising wave of crime and violence. Ramsey Clark, the former United States attorney general, makes this acute observation:

> Crime reflects the character of a people. This is the painful fact we do not want to face. Other premises are easier to accept, other causes are easier to control. There is no simple reform for defective character. It is as stubborn, durable, and strong as ourselves. It is ourselves.[20]

If the church would devote its energies to exposing our people to the means of grace, especially to the gospel of salvation, it would be instrumental in the changing of character, and indirectly it would be contributing to the solution of the problem of crime. This is not to belittle attempts to deal with this problem through tighter laws and more police, but these are staying actions. The real battle is the one that must be waged for the souls of men.

May there arise in our time spiritually disciplined fellowships that will be leaven in the lump, light in the world, the salt of the earth. Nevertheless, such will arouse opposition because there will be a bite or sting in their message and in their actions. But the church needs those who are willing to be sheep among wolves, who are not afraid of being exiles in this world. The future belongs to those who are willing to stand against the spirit of the times (*Zeitgeist*) and bear the cross in costly discipleship. Such persons will be signs and witnesses of the kingdom that has dawned in Jesus Christ and that will be consummated when he comes again.

The great need today is for meaning and purpose. Theologians like Tillich and psychiatrists like Victor Frankl contend that the modern age is afflicted with the anxiety of meaninglessness and rootlessness. Through fulfilling its uniquely spiritual mission the church can do more to effect social change than by proposing social programs and blueprints for a new society. Behind all lasting social reformation is spiritual transformation.

An examination of history will bear out this premise. It can be shown that the great shapers and movers of culture were the prophets and saints of religion. Even those who chose the pathway of flight from the world exerted a far greater influence than those who accommodated and made their peace with the mood of the times.

In the fifteenth century we can point to Nicholas of Flüe or "Brother Claus" who became a hermit in the mountains of Switzerland, yet he changed the whole course of Swiss history. He was consistently sought out as an advisor by political leaders of the Swiss confederacy and was responsible for turning them away from an imperialistic path and laying the foundation for Swiss neutralism. He was also instrumental in reconciling the Swiss leaders and saving his country from civil war. Yet his life was dedicated to prayer in a mountain hermitage.

Other Catholic saints and mystics who had an expressly religious vocation but who helped change history were Ambrose of Milan, Bernard of Clairvaux, Gregory the Great, Francis of Assisi, Teresa of Avila, Catherine of Siena, and Ignatius Loyola. Some of these were inadvertently involved in politics, but they did not seek to be political theologians, for their primary mission was to save souls.

At the time of the Reformation we can mention any of the great Reformers as effecters of social change, but let us give special attention to John Knox. This famed Scottish Reformer attacked the evil in that land with the sword of the Spirit.

He constantly sought men out, whether nobles, peasants, or princes and pressed upon them the claims of Christ. It was said of him at his death: "There lies he who never feared the face of man." He feared only God, and this is why he was fearless in calling men in high places to account before God. Out of his preaching men's hearts were changed, and when men's hearts are changed, nations change. From the new spiritual vision there came a political and social revolution which saw Scotland win its independence.

Mention might also be made of John Wesley who by his revivals saved England from the revolution of violence that tore France asunder. This is indeed the position of such renowned historians as William Lecky and Elie Halévy.[21] In addition the evangelical awakenings in England resulted in a growing abhorrence of the slave trade, and evangelicals of the Clapham Sect were chiefly responsible for getting laws passed that did away with this obnoxious practice. They also saw to it that the national lottery was abolished as well as bull-baiting and cock-fighting.[22]

In America it was John Woolman, the Quaker evangelist, who aroused the conscience of society by his denunciation of the slave trade and who was instrumental in getting slavery abolished in the Quaker communion. He gave away his own slaves, and though he was not active politically, by his example he made a lasting impression upon many people. Indeed, it can be said that he planted the seeds of the abolitionist movement. It is interesting to observe that Thomas Jefferson, a contemporary of Woolman, though noted as a liberal statesman and child of the Enlightenment, retained his household slaves and had benighted private views on race.[23]

A striking example in our own time of an effecter of social change is Commissioner Charles Péan of the Salvation Army in France. He admirably combined evangelism, social service, and political action. In addition to ministering to the spiritual and physical needs of the convicts on Devil's Island off French Guiana for more than twenty years, he was instrumental in bringing back 5000 prisoners to France under Salvation Army parole supervision. He also aroused the citizenry of France by his social protests until the French government was forced to close permanently this cruel and inhuman penal island in 1954. Péan saw, however, that only the power of the Spirit of God can renew the hearts of condemned prisoners and hardened criminals. "No guards, no psychologists, no counselors, no reformers—nothing but the power of God can change a hardened criminal into a good member of society."[24] What prisoners and criminals most need is the word of salvation, the hope of regeneration, but these must be regarded not as a substitute for social and penal reform but as their basis and goal.

It was through faith that the saints of the Old Testament conquered kingdoms and enforced justice (cf. Heb. 11:32 f.), and it is through faith that justice can be advanced in society today. James Denney reminds us: "The Church which cultivates in all its members the spirit of humanity, the spirit of liberty, justice, generosity, and mercy, will do more for the coming of God's kingdom than if it plunged into the thick of every conflict, or offered its mediation in every dispute."[25] The church can remain silent in the face of social evils only at its peril, but at the same time it must always recognize that it can ill afford to dictate policy to the government and that its chief mission is to remold and reshape the spirits of men. Thus, indirectly, it will be contributing to a more just society. The church is the creator of new men, and new men are moved to create a new social order.

Only Jesus Christ can change the world, but he will not do so in a final and irrevocable way until he comes again in power and glory. Yet even now by his Holy Spirit he is working changes in the midst of society through his ambassadors and servants. Scripture tells us that in the course of world history Satan will be bound for a time (Rev. 20:2), and this means that the Christian can look forward to the fulfillment of many of God's promises even in this present age. To be sure, the justice that we can achieve will be only proximate and relative, and yet there is always room for much improvement. Society can now be changed relatively just as men can be changed relatively. Laws backed by force will always be necessary to guard against the outbreaking of sin, but Christian freedom is already now a viable possibility, and this means that works of love can be performed that go beyond the law. Such works anticipate and witness to the final work of redemption at the end of the age. By looking forward to this time we derive the motivation and power to overcome evil and conquer the world for Jesus Christ.

NOTES

1. Quoted in N. B. Stonehouse, *J. Gresham Machen* (Grand Rapids: Eerdmans, 1954), p. 187.

2. See, e.g., John M. Swomley, Jr., *Liberation Ethics* (New York: Macmillan Co., 1972).

3. Jaroslav Pelikan, ed., *Luther's Works*, Vol. 29 (St. Louis: Concordia, 1968), p. 57.

4. For a current and illuminating discussion of this parable see Duane H. Thebau, "On Separating Sheep From Goats" in *Christianity Today*, Vol. XVI, No. 22 (Aug. 11, 1972), pp. 4, 5.

5. P. T. Forsyth, *The Soul of Prayer* (Grand Rapids: Eerdmans, n.d.), p. 16.

6. Rudolf Bultmann, *Faith and Understanding* (London: SCM Press, 1969), p. 111. John Howard Yoder errs in the opposite direction in seeing Jesus' message as essentially political and social. See his *The Politics of Jesus* (Grand Rapids: Eerdmans, 1972).

7. James Kallas, *The Significance of the Synoptic Miracles* (Greenwich, Conn.: Seabury Press, 1961).

8. Alan Richardson, "Poor" in Alan Richardson, ed., *Theological Word Book of the Bible* (New York: Macmillan, 1960), pp. 168, 169.

9. To the credit of Cone he seeks to maintain continuity with the message of the Bible. This is not true of William R. Jones who frankly espouses secular humanism as the only viable philosophical basis for black liberation. See his *Is God a White Racist? A Preamble to Black Theology* (Garden City, N.Y.: Doubleday, 1973).

10. *Luther's Works*, Vol. 45, (Phil.: Muhlenberg Press, 1962), p. 264. At the same time Luther contended that the Christian cause cannot be furthered by force, particularly where this involves resistance to the governing powers. "For one must not resist the government with force, but only with knowledge of the truth; if not, you are innocent, and suffer wrong for God's sake." WML, III, 269. Quoted in Jaroslav Pelikan, ed., *Interpreters of Luther* (Philadelphia: Fortress, 1968), p. 57.

Ellul would be in general agreement with Luther's pessimistic portrayal of the state, but he holds that Christians should not participate in those political roles where the use of force is necessitated. We maintain against Ellul that in some circumstances Christians may do so but with an uneasy conscience.

11. Colin Morris, British Methodist clergyman, speaks of salvation through violent revolution and hails Jesus as a political insurrectionist in his *Unyoung—Uncolored—Unpoor* (Nashville: Abingdon Press, 1969). For a quite different approach by a scholar who sees Jesus as standing against the violent resistance movement see Martin Hengel, *Victory Over Violence* (Philadelphia: Fortress, 1973).

12. Jacques Ellul, *Violence*, trans. Cecelia Gaul Kings (New York: Seabury Press, 1969), p. 138.

13. Quoted in *The Christian Century*, Vol. LXXXVIII, No. 49 (Dec. 8, 1971), pp. 1437, 1438.

14. Jean Lasserre, *War and the Gospel* (Scottdale, Pa.: Herald Press, 1962). In my opinion this is the best defense of pacifism from a biblical and Reformed perspective that is currently available.

15. I here concur with Vernard Eller in his illuminating *King Jesus' Manual of Arms for the Armless* (Nashville: Abingdon, 1973), though unlike Eller I believe that responsible political involvement presupposes and sanctions the use of force in maintaining order in society.

16. *Christian Life*, Vol. 32, No. 2 (June, 1970), p. 58.

17. See Donald G. Bloesch, *Wellsprings of Renewal: Promise in Christian Communal Life* (Grand Rapids: Eerdmans, 1974).

18. Johannes Verkuyl, *Break Down the Walls*, trans. Lewis Smedes (Grand Rapids: Eerdmans, 1973), p. 55.

19. Emmanuel Mounier, "Christian Faith and Civilization" in his *The Spoil of the Violent* (West Nyack, New York: *Cross Currents* Reprint, 1961), p. 15.

20. Ramsey Clark, *Crime in America* (New York: Simon & Schuster, 1970), p. 15. While concurring with Clark that poor living conditions accentuate the propensity to crime, I do not agree that "the solutions for our slums, for racism and crime itself . . . are basically economic" (p. 67).

21. Bernard Semmel gives current credence to this thesis in his *The Methodist Revolution* (New York: Basic Books, 1973).

22. See Ian Bradley, " 'Saints' Against Sin" in *Christianity Today*, Vol. XVII, No. 18 (June 8, 1973), pp. 15, 16.

23. Jefferson nonetheless advanced a bill in the Virginia House of Burgesses which would have allowed owners of slaves to free them. Also his 1778 bill banned the further importation of slaves into Virginia. See *The Progressive* (Nov., 1972), p. 16.

24. In *Chicago Tribune* (Sept. 9, 1972), Section I, p. 8. See Charles Péan, *Devil's Island* (London: Hodder and Stoughton, 1939).

25. James Denney, *Studies in Theology* (London: Hodder and Stoughton, 1895), p. 201.

Index of Names

Index of Subjects

94020